MARRIED TO THE MAFIA DON

A Forced Marriage Italian Mafia Romance

MARIA FROST

Sloane Cameron Publishing

Trigger Warnings

Married to the Mafia Don contains the following tropes and potential triggers:

Tropes:

- Forced marriage
- Virgin heroine
- Touch her and die
- Who hurt you?
- Italian Mafia
- OTT jealous/possessive hero
- Age gap
- He falls first
- Hero has a cat
- Pregnancy

Potential Triggers:

- Cursing

- Sex on the page
- Violence on the page
- Death of minor characters
- Domestic abuse
- Suicide

ONE

Kelsey

———————

"I'm sorry, Dad," I cry, cowering on the floor as his hands curl into fists above my head.

"You can't even get my dinner right!" he roars. "What the fuck is wrong with you?"

His face looms down, inches from mine, beer fumes wafting from his open mouth as he continues to yell at me.

I'm exhausted and starving, too tired to fight as he grabs me and drags me through to the kitchen.

"What is that?" he asks, shoving my face toward the acrid stench of my sin.

"Your supper," I reply, feeling the roaring heat getting far too close to my cheek. "Please, you're hurting me, Dad."

"Burnt to cinders." He spits into the pot on the stove. "You think we can afford to waste food in this house? Think I spend all day slaving so you can burn through my money?"

"I'm sorry, Dad," I reply, my voice trembling. "I'll make it again."

"Like fuck you will," he replies, letting go of me so he can point at the pot. "That is your supper for the next two days. Maybe the taste will remind you to do a better job next time."

He's raising his fist to hit me again when a sharp knock on the front door makes him pause. He suddenly looks terrified. I've never seen him look afraid before. "Find out who that is," he hisses, shoving me toward the door, "and get rid of them."

I rush to answer as there's another loud knock. My heart pounds as I weave between the piles of tottering garbage. I hope it's a neighbor or a delivery, anything to delay the inevitable beating that's only just begun.

As I pull open the door, my heart comes to a standstill, my throat turning dry.

A man stands there. Not just any man. This God is at least a foot taller than me. He's dressed in a perfectly tailored suit that exudes power and control. His jet black hair frames chiseled features, and his eyes, cold and piercing, send a shiver down my spine.

Behind him stand two other men, equally intimidating despite their shorter stature. They all radiate a menacing aura, making it clear they are men who kill as easily as they speak.

"Good evening," the giant says, his voice smooth and controlled, rumbling deep, with a slight Italian accent. "I'm looking for a Mr. Dawson. Is he here?"

I swallow hard, trying to keep my voice steady. "He's out," I reply, the practiced lie rolling straight off my tongue. "Preaching the Lord's work to the masses."

The man's smile is thin, almost predatory. "You are a poor liar." He leans past me. "Dawson, don't make your daughter cover for you. Your car's out front, you dumb bastard."

My father staggers through from the kitchen, his face pale and drawn. "Don Rossi," he says, his voice dripping with fear. "So good to see you in person."

"Call me Marcus. We're all friends here after all, aren't we? I'll call you Gabriel, shall I?"

"Of course, Marcus. Anything you say, Marcus. Kelsey, go to your room. This doesn't involve you."

Marcus steps forward, placing one enormous hand on my shoulder in a strangely possessive gesture. "She stays."

My father nods, defeat settling into his posture. "Don't make her watch you kill me, please."

"Who said anything about killing? Let's sit." The two bodyguards remain at the doorway, one looking in, the other out into the street.

Marcus follows us into the lounge where my father collapses onto the couch. "I can't get it back," Dad says, picking up his beer can and draining the contents. "Hawke's already got it."

"Gabriel," the man says, his tone devoid of sympathy, "You owe me a substantial debt."

My father looks up, his eyes red-rimmed and spiteful. "What do you want me to say? It's gone, I told you. If you're here to kill me, get on with it before my hangover kicks in."

Marcus's smile is cold. "How much did he pay you to steal it?"

"Five thousand."

Marcus's eyes narrow. "You're a competent thief but a foolish negotiator. It was worth fifty on the open market. Priceless to me, but that's another matter."

Dad sags lower, letting out a groan. "You're fucking kidding me." He shakes his head. "So the asshole cheated me. I'm supposed to be part of the Hawke famiglia and this is how he treats me?"

"You're not a made man. You never killed anyone. You're a hired hand for a prick, that's all."

Marcus starts counting on his fingers. "Let me see if I've got this right. One, you run up a significant debt at my bookmakers because Hawke won't let you gamble at his establishments anymore. Two, you steal from me knowing how I treat thieves. Three, you haven't even been paid, have you?"

"How did you know?"

"Because if you had the five thousand, I'd have found you drunk in a bar, not sitting at home surrounded by boxes of stolen goods."

Dad shakes his head. "He said he'd have it for me tomorrow."

"You won't see a penny." Marcus folds his arms. "You owe me a debt and you stole from me. That is unforgivable."

Dad shifts in his seat, sweat pouring down his face. "Look, I'm sorry, okay? Maybe I can get it back from him, I know where he's keeping it. Just give me a chance."

Marcus shakes his head slowly, pulling a gun from inside his jacket as he looks my way for the first time. "Say goodbye to your father."

TWO

Kelsey

Panic surges through me as he points the gun at Dad's head. I throw myself in front of my father, arms spread wide. "No! Please, don't kill him. I'll do anything."

Marcus shakes his head. "Move aside."

"Please, don't kill him, I'm begging you."

A smile flickers across his lips. "A brave girl to fight a mafia boss."

My blood goes cold. "You're in the mafia?"

Dad snorts. "He isn't in the mafia. He runs the fucking New York mafia. Hawke's empire is half the size of Marcus's."

Marcus nods. "He's not wrong. You willing to die for your father?

"I'll do whatever it takes to clear his debt. Just don't kill him."

He takes hold of my wrist, twisting it to expose the bruises on my forearm. "Why would you defend a man who keeps you in squalor? Who gave you these bruises?"

"Because he's my father."

"Bullshit. There's got to be more to it than that."

"I promised my mom I'd take care of him, okay. Before she died I said I'd look after him."

"How old were you when you made such a foolish promise?

"Twelve. Why?"

"And how old are you now?"

"Twenty-one. What does it matter?"

Marcus's eyes narrow as he studies me. "So to honor your oath to your mother, you'll do anything to save your father's life?"

I nod, tears pricking my eyes. "Just don't hurt him. He's the only family I've got left."

A flicker of something—respect, perhaps—crosses Marcus's face. He lowers the gun, but his expression remains cold. "Very well. I won't kill him. I'll marry you instead."

My father gasps, the beer can falling from his hand, foam spreading across the stained floor.

Marcus stares at me so intensely I feel like I'm naked in front of him. "You have three minutes to pack your things." He taps his watch. "Get moving. Anything left behind is gone for good."

"Just promise me you won't hurt him."

Marcus's smile widens, a flicker of satisfaction in his eyes. "Your father will be safe as long as you accept your fate. Two minutes fifty."

I turn and hurry to my room. As I run my eyes over my few belongings, I overhear their conversation through the thin walls.

"You're lucky your daughter cares so much about you," Marcus is saying, his voice cold.

"That's how I've brought her up," my father replies, smugness lacing his words. "We take care of each other in our family."

Marcus retorts sharply. "And the rags she's wearing? The bruises? Is that how you take care of her?"

My hands tremble as I reach for my few clothes, stuffing them into a worn bag.

Dad is sounding more like his usual self. "You don't know what it's like. She needs a firm hand or she'd walk all over me. It was the same with her mother. You either control women or they control you."

"Is that right?"

"You're a mob boss. You know what it's like. Take control or be controlled."

"You feel like you're in control, Gabriel?"

I grab the only photo I have of my mother, her gentle smile making me want to cry. I add the medical textbook that belonged to her. Lastly, I take the small, battered teddy bear she gave me for my third birthday.

I can almost feel the weight of Marcus's next words. "A real father takes care of his children, he doesn't beat them or dress them in rags."

"It's all right for you. You've got millions. Perfect childhood, no doubt. Now judging others. We're barely scraping by here. Am I supposed to buy her new clothes all the fucking time? How am I supposed to afford that?"

"You can afford beer, I notice. Making bets every night of the week. Where's the money come from for that little pastime?"

"You'd drink if you had to raise a kid on your own. You don't get it. I buy her new shit, and the next week she wants more. This way, she doesn't get ideas above her station. And if I have to slap her to keep her in line, that's just life, isn't it? My dad kicked the shit out of me far worse than she ever gets it. She's got nothing to complain about."

"You let her work?"

"Sure, until she got her useless ass fired last week."

I zip my bag closed. Dad's missing a big part of the story out. I was fired because my boss touched me up and all the anger I feel toward my father came spilling out and I slapped the son of a bitch. I was out the door two minutes later.

"What job did she do?" Marcus is asking.

"She was a waitress. Look, if I get it back, will you let her go?"

"Will you beat her again if I do?"

"Of course. I'll never hurt her again, I swear."

I step back into the living room as Marcus is grabbing my father by the throat, lifting him into the air. "You're a shitty liar. Touch her again, and I'll kill you with my fucking hands. Is that clear?"

I grab Marcus's huge arm, trying to yank it back down. "Please," I say as Dad turns purple. "You're killing him. You promised."

Marcus loosens his grip. Dad falls to the ground, gasping for air. "You're a psycho," Dad wheezes, eyes bulging.

Marcus smiles coldly back at him. "And I'm also your daughter's new husband."

THREE

Marcus
_____

I glance over at Kelsey. She sits rigidly next to me, her hands clasped tightly in her lap, eyes wide with fear as she stares at the front of the limo.

Tony's driving, Alex to my right, both ready for any trouble.

Her clothes are filthy, nothing but torn rags. Still, she tries to keep herself clean. Her hair's free of knots, tied neatly back behind her head, her skin glows with radiance.

As I watch, I notice she's shivering.

I tap the button beside me, increasing the heat a few degrees.

Her stomach growls loudly.

"Hungry?" I ask.

She flinches, her eyes darting to mine and then away again, like she thinks I'm about to hit her. My heart aches as I want to take her pain away, wrap my arms around her, tell her no one will ever hurt her again.

I don't do it. Emotions are weaknesses. Vulnerabilities to be exploited. No one exploits me and lives.

"Answer me," I command.

"I... I'm fine," she replies hesitantly.

I watch her for a moment, memories of my own childhood flashing through my mind. The beatings, the hunger, the desperate need for someone, anyone, to protect me from my father. I push the thoughts aside, keeping my expression neutral.

"Bullshit," I say. "You're half starved. Your father clearly doesn't feed you too well. I'm guessing he spends it all on booze and gambling. Took all your waitressing money, I bet."

"He looks after me okay."

"You don't need to lie. He can't hurt you anymore." I tap the intercom. "Tony, take us to La Fontaine."

"What's that?" she asks as the limo takes a right.

"Couple of Michelin stars. Six month waiting list. Best meatballs in Manhattan. You'll love it."

"I'm not exactly dressed for fine dining, am I?" she mutters, looking down at her clothes.

"That can be resolved easily enough."

She lapses into silence. "It's funny, isn't it?" I continue, my voice edged with a dark humor.

"What is?"

"I came to your house to kill your father and now I'm going to marry you. I never would have predicted that."

"Funny?" she asks bitterly, her eyes flashing with anger. "What's the amusing part? Almost murdering my dad or kidnapping me?"

"I just mean fate clearly had plans for us both today. That thought tickles me, that's all," I say, trying to keep my tone light but feeling the weight of her words. "If you'd not been home, he'd be dead."

"Well, forgive me for not laughing," she snaps, "but I don't find that remotely funny." She crosses her arms defensively.

"You want to go back to him? To that life?" I ask, frustration creeping into my voice. "You saying you want that?"

"Are you saying life with you will be any better?" She retorts, her voice dripping with sarcasm. "You're a mobster. Am I meant to be happy I'm being forced to marry you?"

"You're meant to be grateful I removed you from that miserable life," I reply, my tone hardening. "I can give you anything you want, Kelsey. All you have to do is stick my ring on your finger. Is that such a big deal?"

"At least with my father, I knew what to expect. I saw the way he looked at you. He was terrified. That can't be for no reason."

"You're underestimating what I can offer you," I say, stepping closer. "Freedom, power, respect. All you have to do is trust me."

"Trust you?" she scoffs, taking a step back. "How can I trust someone who solves all his problems with a gun?"

"I do what I have to do to survive," I snap. "This world isn't kind, Kelsey. You either take control of it or you get trampled by it." I wince inwardly as I think how close I am to mirroring her father's words. Am I no different to him?

"Maybe I don't want to live in a world where that's the only choice," she fires back, her voice trembling slightly.

I soften my tone, sensing her vulnerability. "I'm not asking you to love me or even like me. I'm asking you to give this a chance. You might find it's not as bad as you think. I'll control everything, you'll never worry about anything again."

She looks at me, her eyes searching mine, conflicted. "I don't want to be controlled," she says quietly.

"And I don't want to control you," I reply, surprising myself with the honesty in my voice. "I want a partner, not a prisoner. But you have to meet me halfway."

She hesitates, the defiance in her eyes warring with something else—something softer. "I don't know if I can do that," she whispers.

As she turns away, I feel a strange mix of frustration and hope. This woman, with her fiery spirit and unyielding defiance, is going to be the challenge of my life. And for some reason, that thought excites me.

"Why'd you get fired?" I ask.

"Because my boss tried to cop a feel and I slapped him for it. Want to give it a try? I'm happy to give you a demonstration."

She turns away again. Her shoulders start to shake and I

know why. She's crying silently, hoping I won't notice. I could comfort her but I don't want another fight.

She's lashing out because she's never been able to before. That's understandable. I got into fights every time my dad kicked the shit out of me. I used to go looking for trouble, drive to Hawke's patch, find any of his men I could and kick the shit out of them. It's how you let off steam.

She intrigues me. There's beauty in her face, but so much pain there too. She's clearly been put through the mill by her father but he's not doused her fire entirely. I see sparks of something in her eyes, something I recognize from my own youth. She's got dreams, not quite crushed. I wonder what they are.

She doesn't turn around again until we reach the restaurant.

The limo door is opened by the valet. His eyes widen as he recognizes me. He quickly composes himself as I step out. "Don Rossi," he says, his voice filled with fear as my bodyguards climb out of the front. "How good to see you again."

I ignore him, extending a hand to Kelsey. She takes it reluctantly but as our fingers touch, I see her pupils dilate. Her heart is racing, no doubt.

She wants me. Not surprising, most women do. But I don't want most women. Hell, I haven't fucked anyone in years. So why does her touch make me want to bend her over the car hood and rip her panties off? Even when she looks at me like she wants to slit my throat, I still want to fuck the hell out of her.

"This way," I tell her, keeping hold of her hand as I lead her inside, my bodyguards following close behind.

The place is packed with the lunchtime crowd. Crystal chandeliers hang from the ceiling, casting a warm glow over the plush, richly decorated interior.

The scent of exquisite cuisine fills the air, mingling with the soft murmur of conversation. Until we enter. Patrons and staff alike freeze at the sight of me, their eyes widening in a mix of fear and awe. There's not a sound to be heard in the entire place.

The maître d' hurries over, his face pale. "Mr. Rossi, welcome," he stammers. "It is truly an honor to have you here again. Your usual table?"

"A private room this time, Francis," I reply, observing the discomfort in Kelsey's eyes as she feels eyes on her from all around.

"Of course. This way."

We pass tables where the diners whisper behind their hands, their gazes darting away when I meet their eyes. It's a familiar reaction, one I've cultivated over the years. Power is best wielded when it's both seen and feared. I've helped many people in this restaurant at one time or another, threatened many more.

We reach the private room, but it's already occupied. A group of men sit around the table, their laughter and conversation halting abruptly as we enter.

The maître d' whispers urgently to them, and one by one, they rise to leave, their complaints dying on their lips as they recognize me. All except one – a drunk who remains seated, back to me, oblivious to who I am, too hammered to realize how close he is to death.

"I'm not going anywhere," he slurs. "Just because some rich asshole wants this place, tell him to go fuck himself. I booked it for my bachelor party eight months ago and I'm not about to–" His head twists and as he sees me, the words fade away. His face turns pale as a dark spot appears on the front of his pants. "Don Rossi," he mutters, swallowing hard. "I'm sorry. Please, I meant no disrespect."

"Leave," I say. "Now."

I turn to Kelsey as he sprints for the door. "Take a seat," I tell her.

"I don't belong here," she whispers as I hold a chair out for her.

"Take a look at the menu," I command, my tone firm but not unkind. "I'll be back shortly. My bodyguards will keep you safe. Size six, right?"

"What?"

"Prefer flats or heels?"

"I've never worn heels in my life."

"Flats it is then."

FOUR

Marcus

I step out of the restaurant, crossing the street toward a high-end clothing store. There's a dress in the window that would look perfect shredded to pieces on my bedroom floor.

Inside, the clerk looks up, startled but quickly masking her surprise. "May I help you, Don Rossi?" she asks, thrusting her chest toward me.

"I need clothes for a woman, size ten. Something elegant. Suitable for dinner. Make it snappy."

She returns with an array of expensive outfits. "Any of these would be suitable, I think. Would you like to look through them?"

"Do you sell wedding dresses?" I ask, an idea occurring to me.

"We don't, I'm afraid." She hands me a business card. "But here's the number for Laura White. She's very good. She made mine."

"Thank you," I say, pocketing the card.

She smiles flirtatiously up at me. "I'm divorced now though."

I don't return the smile. "Send the outfits to my penthouse."

"Which ones?"

"All of them." I take a red dress from her arms. "Except this one. I'll take this now."

"Of course, Don Rossi. Whatever you say."

"I need flats, size six, to match the dress."

Two minutes later, I'm back in La Fontaine, handing the dress and a matching pair of shoes to Kelsey. "Go change in the restroom," I instruct.

She takes it, her eyes wary, and heads to the restroom without arguing, shoulders slumped. I turn to Alex, handing him the business card. "Arrange a wedding venue for Saturday. Give this woman a call, get a dress sorted."

"What about the necklace?" Tony asks.

I give him a cold smile. "Dawson gets it back or he dies trying. Either way, I win."

"You know Hawke only ordered the theft to fuck with you. What if he sells it? Or destroys it?"

I shake my head. "He knows it belonged to my grand-mother. It only gives him leverage over me if he has it in his possession. Mark my words, sooner or later he'll want to talk partnership."

"And I thought he took it because you killed Reggie."

"Reggie was a cruel little prick. Kicked the shit out of three hookers before I got hold of him."

Alex shrugs. "Blood's blood though, isn't it? You killed Hawke's nephew. Couldn't have expected him to take it lying down?"

I clench my fists. "You saying I deserved to get the necklace stolen?"

"No, boss. I'm saying maybe you should have had the alarms upgraded, knowing he might want revenge for Reggie."

Tony glares at him. "We were expecting a firebombing, not a thief sneaking in to steal one necklace during a party. You want to be in charge?"

"Shut up bickering," I tell them. "What's done is done. All I care about is getting it back."

I glance at my watch. Kelsey has had long enough. I walk over to the restroom and shove the door open.

She's struggling to open the locked window at the back, the dress and shoes forgotten on the floor behind her. She freezes when she hears me come in.

"I'm curious," I say, my tone cold as she turns back around. "Where would you go? Back to him?"

"I don't know," she snaps, her shoulders slumping as she turns to face me. "But I can't stay here with you. You're a criminal."

"So's your dear old daddy. Now, we made a deal. Unless you want me to go back to your place and shoot pops in the head, go in that cubicle right fucking now and get changed." I pick up the dress and hold it out to her. "You have one minute." I step back, watching her walk into the nearest cubicle with the dress over her arm.

"I know you don't want to marry me," I say as the door locks. "But you need to get used to the idea. It's happening whether you like it or not."

The door opens again and she comes out looking fucking gorgeous. "Why do you want to marry me anyway?" she asks. "What's in it for you?"

"I've bought you clothes, cleared your father's debt, let him live, and freed you from that awful house. Now I'm buying you lunch. Would being my wife really be that bad?"

"You're not answering my question."

"I need an heir for my empire," I explain simply. "I'm not getting any younger."

"There's a million women out there. Go choose one of them."

"I don't want them. I want you."

She scoffs. "You don't know a thing about me."

"Tell me then," I challenge. "Who are you, Kelsey? What do you want out of life?"

She hesitates, then starts speaking, her voice softer than before. "To be a doctor."

"Why?"

"My mom was training to be one. That was how she met my dad. She was treating him and he charmed her, that's how she described it. She never did become a doctor. He soon stopped all that. Got her pregnant with me and made her quit college. I want to finish what she started."

I nod. "If you give me an heir, I will pay for your medical degree." I reach out and touch her hand, my grip firm and possessive. "Think about it," I add. "You get your dream and I get my heir. We both win."

She shakes her head. "What if I don't want to raise a child with a criminal?"

"You forget that you already exchanged your hand for your father's life. If you prefer, I could go back and kill him and you could continue living in that shithole all on your lonesome."

She turns pale, shaking her head. "Don't kill him," she mutters. "Please. You promised."

I smile coldly. "And so did you. We're getting married, and then I'm fucking you over and over again until you're pregnant with my heir."

FIVE

Kelsey

The soft hum of the elevator is the only sound. As we ascend to his penthouse, I steal a glance at Marcus from the corner of my eye.

I feel full of food for the first time in months, maybe years. The meal was so good and all paid for by the man staring in front of him, saying nothing.

Dressed in a perfectly tailored suit, he towers over me, exuding an air of dominance that is both alluring and terrifying.

His dark hair is neatly styled, accentuating the sharp lines of his chiseled jaw and high cheekbones. God, he looks so good.

This close, I can see hints of salt and pepper, the only real signs of his age. His eyes, a piercing blue, are cold and calculating, yet there's a smoldering intensity behind them that makes my pulse race.

He's undeniably handsome, but there's an edge to him that scares the shit out of me.

His presence is magnetic, drawing me in despite the fear that grips my heart. I can feel the heat of his body, the sheer force of his personality radiating off him in waves. It's impossible to ignore him, impossible to pretend that he doesn't affect me.

I want to hate him, to focus on the terror he instills in me, but there's a part of me that can't help but be grateful. He saved me from my father's clutches, bought me new clothes, paid for the best meal I've ever eaten, and even threatened my father for hurting me.

How can I hate a man who did what no one else ever did for me? Who scared my father? Who protected me when he didn't even know a thing about me?

The elevator doors slide open with a soft chime, revealing the opulent penthouse. "The elevator goes straight into your place?" I ask as I step out. The space is breathtaking, with floor-to-ceiling windows offering a panoramic view of the city lights.

"My building," he replies. "My elevator. Make yourself at home."

Everything is immaculate, from the plush carpets to the expensive artwork adorning the walls. Yet, it feels impersonal, more like a showpiece than a home.

Marcus's hand gently touches the small of my back, guiding me forward. His touch sends a shiver down my spine, a reminder of the power he holds over me.

I glance up at him, my heart pounding in my chest. His expression is unreadable, his eyes scanning the room as if assessing its safety. He looks down at me, his gaze softening for a brief moment.

"Still rather be back him with?" he asks, his voice smooth and commanding.

My mouth is dry, and my thoughts are a jumble of fear and confusion. I follow him into the living room, my fingers clutching the soft fabric of the gorgeous dress he bought me.

It's beautiful, more luxurious than anything I've ever owned, but it feels like a costume, a disguise hiding the reality of my situation.

He stops in the center of the room and turns to face me. "Take a shower," he instructs, his tone leaving no room for argument. "Time for a fresh start, don't you think? Pajamas are on their way up. I'll bring them to you."

I nod again, too exhausted to protest. The events of the day have left me drained, both physically and emotionally. I head towards the bathroom, my steps unsteady.

The bathroom is as luxurious as the rest of the penthouse, with gleaming marble and high-end fixtures. I undress and step into the shower, letting the hot water cascade over me. For a brief moment, I allow myself to relax, the warmth soothing my aching muscles.

But then, I see movement across the room. Panic surges through me, and I scream as something darts toward me. My first thought is that it's a rat. I've seen enough in my time to know to react quickly. No, it's too big to be a rat. What the hell is that?

The door bursts open, and Marcus rushes in, gun in hand as I brandish a shampoo bottle in front of me.

"Over there," I say, pointing toward the corner of the room. He looks, his eyes narrowing until he spots the source of my terror. A cat dashes from the room.

"You've met the landlord," Marcus says, holstering the gun with a smirk as his eyes run down my naked body. "I wondered where he'd got to. Housekeeper usually lets him nap in the laundry room."

"Very funny." I feel his eyes on my bruises, and I grab a towel and wrap it around me. "What's a cat doing in here anyway?"

"I told you. He owns the place. I just rent a bedroom from him."

He walks out, returning a moment later with a bundle of clean clothes. He steps close, his presence overwhelming in the small, steamy space. His fingers brush against the bruises on my arms and shoulders.

"You should let me call a doctor," he says softly, his touch lingering on a particularly dark bruise. "Get you checked over."

I pull back, hugging the towel tighter around me. "I'm fine," I snap, though the warmth of his fingers and the concern in his voice make my heart race for reasons I don't want to acknowledge. My emotions are a tangled mess of fear, anger, and an attraction I wish I didn't feel.

He doesn't argue, but his eyes linger on me, a mixture of frustration and something softer. For a moment, I almost wish he would take me in his arms, hold me, and tell me everything will be okay. But then I remember who he is, and the moment passes.

"Come out when you're dressed," he says, his voice returning to its usual commanding tone. "I'll distract him so he doesn't go for your jugular."

I wait until he leaves the bathroom before I open the bag. The pajamas inside are made of soft, luxurious silk, a pale lavender color that shimmers in the light.

The top is a delicate camisole with thin straps and a low neckline, barely covering my breasts. The matching shorts are tiny, hugging my hips and leaving most of my legs exposed. I feel naked just looking at them, but I have no other option.

I dress quickly, feeling the cool fabric slide over my skin, making me shiver. The camisole clings to my curves, the silk so thin that my nipples are clearly visible through the fabric.

The shorts ride up with every movement, making me acutely aware of how exposed I am. I take a deep breath, trying to steel myself, and step out of the bathroom.

Marcus is waiting for me in the living room, the cat purring contentedly on his lap. He looks up as I enter, his eyes widening as they take in my appearance. The tension between us is palpable, the air thick with unspoken words.

"You look perfect," he says.

"And you look like a Bond villain," I reply, unable to resist a smile. "Does that wall rotate behind you?"

"Straight into the guest bedroom" he replies, pointing to a door off to the side. "Or you could take the door if you want to be old fashioned."

"The guest bedroom? I thought—"

You thought I'd drag you into my bed like a caveman. Not until we're married. After that, I won't stop fucking you until you're pregnant. Until then, enjoy your solitude."

His words send a shiver down my spine, a mix of fear and a reluctant thrill. How did I end up here, with a man who exudes power and danger, who talks of taking my virginity with such casual confidence? I feel the weight of his gaze on me, both arousing and intimidating.

"Do I get any say in this?" I ask.

"You could refuse to let me but we both know you won't."

"You seem very sure of yourself."

"Your pupils dilate whenever I touch you. Your nipples are rock hard right now. I bet if I touched your pussy, it would be wet, wouldn't it?"

"I'm going to bed," I say, needing to get some distance between us. I can't admit the son of a bitch is right. I'm soaked just thinking of him fucking me.

I turn away from him, my mind buzzing with conflicting thoughts.

The guest bedroom is as luxurious as the rest of the penthouse. The bed is a vast expanse of soft, inviting pillows and silken sheets, almost too perfect to disturb.

The dim lighting casts a warm glow, making the room feel like a safe, cocooned sanctuary. I slip under the covers, feeling the cool fabric against my skin, a soothing contrast to the heat building inside me.

I try to ignore the throbbing sensation between my legs, a persistent reminder of the attraction I feel toward Marcus.

It's overwhelming, a mix of frustration and longing that I can't seem to shake.

Despite my best efforts to push it aside, the desire lingers, growing stronger with each passing second. My mind keeps drifting back to the way Marcus looked at me, the way he touched me, the rough yet gentle timbre of his voice.

I close my eyes, taking a deep breath. I've never been one to give in easily, but the pull is undeniable. It's a new kind of battle, one fought within the confines of my own mind and body.

As much as I want to resist, a part of me craves the release, the escape into fantasy. I tell myself it's okay, that it's natural to explore these feelings and my own body. It's nothing to do with him. It's just scratching an itch, that's all. Helping me get to sleep.

I let my hand slip under the sheets, the fabric whispering softly as I move. My fingers trail along my stomach, the touch light and tentative. I pause, taking another deep breath, trying to relax.

I start by caressing my thighs, the sensation both soothing and electrifying. The gentle strokes help ease some of the tension, allowing me to focus on the sensations rather than the confusion of my emotions.

My fingers trace lazy patterns on my skin, moving higher with each pass. I allow myself to think of Marcus, imagining his hands instead of mine, his voice whispering sweet nothings in my ear.

As my fingers move closer to my core, I feel a jolt of pleasure. I bite my lip, the sensation almost too much to handle. I take a moment to steady my breathing, reminding myself to be gentle.

With a light touch, I start to explore, paying attention to what feels good. I discover that small, circular motions feel best, a delicate dance of pleasure that sends shivers up my spine.

I picture Marcus in my mind, his intense eyes locked on mine, filled with desire. The thought of him watching me, of him knowing exactly what I'm doing, sends a thrill through me.

I imagine his hands on my body, his lips tracing the same path my fingers are taking. The fantasy is intoxicating, blurring the line between reality and imagination.

My touch becomes more confident, more deliberate. I find a rhythm that feels right, slow and steady, allowing the pleasure to build gradually.

It's important to stay relaxed, to keep breathing deeply, and to focus on the sensations rather than rushing to the finish. The slow build-up is key, making the eventual release all the more satisfying. I imagine him watching me, telling me to take my time.

As I continue, I find myself thinking about what it would be like to be with Marcus. The thought of him taking care of me, making sure I feel good, only heightens the pleasure. My hips begin to move in sync with my hand, seeking more friction, more intensity.

I can't help but let out a soft moan, the sound muffled by the pillows. The room feels hot, my skin tingling with every touch. The fantasy becomes more vivid, more real.

I imagine Marcus whispering dirty words in my ear, telling me how beautiful I am, how much he wants me. The thought of him being so close, of his body pressed against mine, is almost too much to bear.

I focus on the sensations, letting the pleasure build and build. It's a slow climb, each touch sending waves of heat through my body. I feel a tension coiling in my lower abdomen, a delicious pressure that signals the approaching climax.

My fingers move faster, the movements more insistent. The fantasy of Marcus's touch, his voice, his presence, consumes me. I imagine his lips on mine, his hands exploring every inch of my body. The thought of him knowing exactly what to do, how to make me feel good, pushes me closer to the edge.

Finally, the tension snaps, and I'm overwhelmed by a wave of pleasure. The orgasm washes over me, intense and all-consuming. I arch my back, my body trembling with the force of it.

"Marcus," I cry out, my hips thrusting into thin air. The sensation is pure bliss, a release of all the pent-up desire and frustration. I bite my lip to keep from crying out, the sound escaping as a soft whimper.

As the pleasure ebbs, I collapse back onto the pillows, breathing heavily. My skin is flushed, my heart pounding in my chest. The room feels cooler now, the air soothing against my overheated skin. I let out a contented sigh, feeling a sense of peace and satisfaction.

For a moment, I just lie there, enjoying the afterglow. The throbbing has subsided, replaced by a pleasant warmth that spreads through my entire body. I feel relaxed, my mind clear and calm.

I can't help but smile. The fantasy of Marcus was intense, almost too real. It makes me wonder about the future, about what could be. But for now, I'm content with the present, with this moment of peace and self-discovery.

I snuggle deeper into the covers, feeling the cool silk against my skin. The room is quiet, the only sound the gentle hum of the city outside. I close my eyes, letting the contentment wash over me.

I carry the memory of the pleasure, the fantasy of Marcus, and the thought that once we're married, it won't just be me touching myself, it'll be him. I fall asleep with a smile on my face.

SIX

Marcus

As I pass by her bedroom, a soft, breathy sound catches my attention. I pause, curiosity piqued. The door is ajar, and through the narrow opening, I catch a glimpse of her.

My breath hitches as I realize she's unaware of my presence. She's lying on the bed, her back arched slightly, one hand resting behind her head while the other seems to be lost between her legs.

Her expression is one of pure vulnerability, a mix of longing and something deeper. The sight of her, so open and unguarded, stirs something within me. I'm captivated, unable to tear my eyes away.

There's an innocence to her movements. It feels intimate, not in a carnal way, but in a deeply personal one. I realize that she's seeking comfort and connection, even if only with herself.

As I stand there, I feel a surge of emotions. Desire, yes, but also a deep, protective tenderness. This woman has come into my life and turned everything upside down.

She's brought light into the dark corners of my world, and I find myself wanting to protect her, to cherish her.

The way her body moves, the soft gasps escaping her lips, it's all so beautiful. I can't help but think about how good her body looked when I walked in on her in the shower earlier.

Her skin, glistening with water, her hair slicked back, the curve of her hips... It's a sight that has been burned into my memory. There's an elegance to her, a grace that draws me in and holds me captive.

She shifts in place and her breathing changes. Her hand moves faster and faster until she thrusts her hips upward. "Marcus," she calls out, falling back onto the bed.

I back away slowly, my cock rock hard. Retreating to my own bedroom, I close the door behind me and lean against it, my mind racing with thoughts of her.

The desire I feel isn't just physical; it's a yearning for connection, for the life we're building together. The way she makes me feel is unlike anything I've ever experienced. It's more than just lust; it's love, respect, and admiration.

I sit on the edge of my bed, the room dimly lit by the city lights streaming through the windows. The image of her, lost in her own pleasure, is still vivid in my mind. It's a moment of pure, unguarded beauty. I long for the day when we can share that intimacy openly, when she'll be mine completely.

As I lie back on the bed, my thoughts are utterly consumed with her. The anticipation of our future together fills me with a warmth I've never experienced before. It's strange how life can take such unexpected turns.

I never envisioned myself as the kind of man who would settle down, let alone dream about starting a family. Yet, here I am, unable to imagine a life without her.

The thought of her pregnant, carrying our child, is a vision that overwhelms me with both tenderness and desire. It's not just the physical aspect that excites me, though the idea of her body changing and growing does stir a deep, primal part of me.

As I think about her, I feel a deep longing to be close to her, to protect her from the chaos and darkness that my world often brings. The memory of her earlier, so open and unguarded, stays with me.

It was a glimpse into her private world, a world I want to be a part of. I think about the times we've shared, the passion and the tenderness, and how those moments have brought us closer together.

There's a raw, magnetic attraction between us, but it's more than that. It's the comfort of knowing she's there for me, the way she makes me feel whole.

The anticipation of seeing her belly grow, knowing that she's nurturing a new life, our life, inside of her—it fills me with a sense of pride and responsibility. I want to be the man who stands by her side through everything, who provides and protects.

I close my eyes, allowing the fantasy to deepen. In my mind's eye, I see us together, her belly swollen with our child, her hand resting on it protectively. She smiles at me, a soft, loving smile that makes my heart swell with pride and affection. I imagine us in a quiet moment, her head resting on my shoulder, my hand on her stomach, feeling the life we created together move inside her.

My mind drifts back to the sight of her naked body when I walked in on her in the shower. The water cascading down her curves, the way her wet hair clung to her skin, the look of surprise in her eyes—it's an image that's hard to shake.

I take my cock in my hand and begin to stroke my shaft, thinking of how she said my name when she came. I close my eyes, imagining her under me, her coming with me inside her, me thrusting deep, getting her pregnant.

It doesn't take me long to come, spurting into empty air. It's the last time. From now on, no cum is wasted. It all goes inside her. I go to sleep with that thought helping a small smile form on my lips.

SEVEN

Kelsey

I wake up in a blind panic. I need to make Dad's breakfast. I slept in. He'll kill him. My heart pounds as I fling my legs out of bed.

But I don't hit splintery floorboards. It's thick soft carpet under my feet. Where the hell am I?

A moment later, it hits me and I relax, my shoulders sagging, my breath hitching.

I'm safe. He can't hit me. He can't yell at me. He can't make me feel like shit anymore.

I'm in Marcus's luxurious penthouse, not my own bed. There's no smell of damp, no sound of my father's snores. I'm not under a single thin mold covered blanket.

I get to my feet and stretch, looking around me. The space is vast and opulent, with high ceilings and floor-to-ceiling windows that offer a breathtaking view of the city below.

But it's also impersonal, like a high-end hotel rather than a home. There are no pictures on the walls, no books on the shelves.

Marcus's nowhere to be seen. I'm guessing he's still asleep.

As I wander through the penthouse, the elevator slides open. My heart skips a beat. Is that Marcus?

No, a man in a chef's uniform stands there, carrying several large bags. He's black, his skin marked with the creases of age, and his short, silver-streaked hair contrasts sharply against the pristine white of his chef's hat.

His face, though weathered, exudes a quiet dignity and kindness, a gentle smile playing at the corners of his mouth as he regards me with a knowing look. He seems indifferent to my tiny pajamas.

His uniform is spotless, the crisp white fabric immaculately pressed, and the embroidered name on his chest reads "Chase."

"Good morning, miss. I'm here to prepare breakfast," he says with a polite smile. "Don Rossi wants you well fed. Chase's the name." He taps the name on his chest.

He moves to the kitchen as if he's been here dozens of times, beginning to unpack his bags. I wonder how many other women Marcus's had here, being cooked breakfast like this.

As he works, the delicious aromas of fresh fruit, pastries, eggs, bacon, smoked salmon, and freshly squeezed orange juice fill the air. My stomach growls loudly, and he chuckles.

"You must be hungry," he says, glancing over at me. "Why

don't you have a seat at the counter? Breakfast will be ready in a few minutes."

I sit down, watching him work. "You're not here every day, are you?" I ask, trying to sound casual.

"No, miss. I only come whenever Mr. Rossi requests it," he replies, focusing on the food. "And before you ask for help getting out of here, that's not going to happen."

I bite my lip, deciding to take the plunge. "How do you know that's what I was going to ask?"

He pauses, looking at me with a mixture of pity and resolve. "Mr. Rossi can find anyone on the planet in fifteen minutes. You'd never get away for long."

"You have to try," I whisper, desperation creeping into my voice. "Please."

He shakes his head, continuing to work. "You're better off accepting the situation. Is it so bad here, Michelin star chef, view of the Hudson people would kill for?"

"But I can't live like this," I insist, my voice trembling. "I have no freedom. He says he's going to marry me, wants to get me pregnant."

He sighs, setting down the knife he's been using. "I've seen what happens to people who cross him. I'm not dying for you. I'm just a chef."

Tears prick at my eyes, but I nod, realizing the futility of arguing. He finishes preparing the food and sets it in front of me. "Please, just eat. Keep your strength up. Trust me, he's not as bad as you think.

"He paid for me to go to catering college when I was forty and fresh out of prison, took me in off the streets, gave me a job. He helps people, even if he never boasts about it. If he wants to marry you, it's because he's seen something in you that you might have missed."

"Like what?"

"Not for me to say."

I start eating, the food tasting like ash in my mouth despite its deliciousness.

He packs up his things and heads to the elevator, giving me a sympathetic look over his shoulder.

I sit there, staring at the doors, feeling the weight of my situation settle heavily on my shoulders. As I look around, I notice the cat from last night prowling around my feet.

I toss him a little piece of salmon. He devours it before jumping onto my lap. I gently scratch behind its ears, finding a small comfort in its purring. The cat's presence is a tiny, welcome distraction from the overwhelming fear and uncertainty I feel.

"Wonder what your name is," I say out loud, continuing to eat and sharing bits of food with the cat.

"Barney," Marcus says, appearing in the doorway out of nowhere.

"Are you a vampire?" I ask. "Where did you come from?"

"All the best Bond villains have secret entrances," he replies.

Behind him I notice several men. Barney darts away, sensing the tension. Marcus looks at me, his gaze piercing and intense.

"He doesn't sit at the table," Marcus replies, his voice calm but authoritative. "But he clearly knows a soft touch when he sees one."

I nod, feeling suddenly vulnerable. "I wasn't the one with him sitting in my lap last night."

He gestures to one of the men, who hands over several bags. Marcus passes them to me. "These will do for now. I'll give you a credit card to get more when you decide what style you like."

I take the bags and look inside, finding a selection of clothes. I pull out a dress that's more revealing than I'm comfortable with, but it's clear I don't have much choice about any of this. The fabric is soft and expensive, the kind of outfit I'd never be able to afford on my own.

"Sticking with the Bond villain vibe," I say, trying to keep my voice steady. "Am I supposed to dangle off your arm and look tittily at your rivals across the baccarat table?"

He shakes his head, tossing me a stack of college brochures. "You're supposed to choose where you want to study medicine."

I stare at him in surprise. I hadn't expected him to keep his word. "You're serious?"

"Of course," he replies. "I always keep my promises."

Despite the luxury and the unexpected kindness, I feel trapped. I struggle with the attraction I feel towards Marcus, hating myself for it. His power over me is palpable, and it scares me. But in my hands are brochures for courses I'd never be able to afford on my own in a million years.

He continues, "I have a meeting. You will go try on some wedding dresses with my bodyguards. You remember Tony and Alex. They'll take care of everything."

The two men step forward from the group, unsmiling as they stare at me. "Such a happy pair," I say. "I'm sure we'll have lots of laughs."

"They're not here to laugh at your jokes, they're here to keep you alive," Marcus replies, his voice smooth and commanding.

I scowl at him, crossing my arms over my chest. "I don't need bodyguards. I need my freedom."

Marcus raises an eyebrow, a smirk playing at the corners of his mouth. "Freedom? Is that what you call living under your father's thumb?"

I grit my teeth, feeling a surge of anger. "At least I wasn't a prisoner trapped a mile above the ground."

"Is that what you think you are now?" he asks, stepping closer, his presence overwhelming. "A prisoner?"

I refuse to back down, lifting my chin defiantly. "What else would you call it?"

He chuckles softly, the sound sending shivers down my spine. "I call it protection. I call it keeping my investment safe. I cleared your father's debts. I bought you and I will keep you safe whether you want me to or not."

"Safe from what?" I snap, hating the way my voice trembles. "From you?"

His eyes darken, his expression turning serious. "Safe from the world I live in. Safe from people who would hurt you to get to me."

I narrow my eyes at him, not wanting to give in. "And what about you, Marcus? What is it you want from me? It can't be just a baby. You could pick any woman in the world."

He moves closer, his hand reaching out to gently touch my cheek. "I don't want them, I want you, same as you want me."

"Bullshit."

"Admit that you're drawn to me."

I slap his hand away, my heart pounding. "You're delusional. I could never be drawn to a man like you."

He laughs, the sound low and dangerous. "You can lie to yourself, Kelsey, but you can't lie to me. I see the way you look at me."

"You see what you want to see," I retort, my voice shaking with a mix of anger and something else I can't quite identify.

His gaze narrows, and he steps even closer, invading my space. "Admit it. You feel something for me."

"It's called contempt," I say, though my voice lacks conviction.

"Is that so?" he murmurs, his breath hot against my ear. "Then why does your pulse race every time I touch you?"

I swallow hard, trying to ignore the heat spreading through my body. "You're imagining things."

He smirks, his lips brushing against my ear as he puts his finger to the pulse point on my wrist. "Am I? Prove it."

I push him away, my hands trembling. "I don't have to prove anything to you."

"Because you can't," he says, his eyes gleaming with triumph. "You're scared of how strongly you feel about me."

"I'm scared of you," I correct, though I know in my heart that is only partly true.

"Good," he says softly, his gaze intense. "Fear can be a powerful motivator."

"I don't want to be motivated by fear," I whisper, hating the vulnerability in my voice.

"Then what do you want to be motivated by?" he asks, his tone challenging.

"By my own choices," I reply, meeting his gaze head-on. "Not by your control."

Marcus's expression softens slightly, and he reaches out to cup my cheek. "You think this is about control?"

"What else could it be?" I whisper, feeling a confusing mix of emotions.

"It's about giving you a life you never had," he says, his voice sincere. "It's about you being free. I'm giving you freedom, even if you don't realize it yet. One day, you'll thank me for this."

I shake my head, tears stinging my eyes. "I don't want to be owned."

"You're not a possession, Kelsey. You're my equal," he murmurs, his thumb brushing away a tear. "But you have to trust me."

"How can I trust you when you've taken everything from me?" I ask, my voice breaking.

"I haven't taken anything," he replies softly. "I've given you freedom from a life of misery."

"You've given me a penthouse with all the doors locked," I say, my voice filled with bitterness.

He sighs, stepping back slightly. "The elevator's open now. You can choose to go, or you can choose to stay and see what we could be."

I stare at him, torn between my fear and the undeniable pull I feel towards him. "Why do you care so much what happens to me?"

"Because you're different," he says simply. "Because I see something in you that I've never seen in anyone else."

"Your chef said the same thing."

"Wise man, that one."

"What do you see in me?" I wince, not sure I want to know the answer. He could break me here, same as my father spent years trying to do.

He puts a hand on my shoulder. "Strength. Courage. A fire that matches my own," he says, his eyes locked onto mine. "You're not just anyone, Kelsey. You're the woman I've chosen. You saved your father. I want that look in your eyes if you get the chance to save me one day."

I take a deep breath, trying to steady my racing heart. "What if I don't want to save you?"

"Then prove it," he challenges, stepping closer again. "Walk away right now."

I hesitate, my mind racing. I want to walk away, to defy him, but something holds me back. I hate him for the power he has over me, but I can't deny the spark of something deeper.

"You can't, can you?" he murmurs, his voice filled with satisfaction as he strokes my cheek.

I glare at him, hating the truth in his words. "This doesn't mean I accept you."

"It means you're considering it," he counters, his gaze softening. "And that's enough for now. Now, go with Tony and Alex and pick a wedding dress."

EIGHT

Kelsey

I stand in the wedding boutique, staring at my reflection in the changing room mirror. The dress is beautiful, delicate lace and satin that make me look like someone else entirely. Someone who isn't trapped in this nightmare.

The bodice fits snugly, cinching my waist and flowing down into a cascade of shimmering fabric. I barely recognize myself. It fits perfectly, like this was meant to be.

Laura, the owner of the boutique, steps back from me. "You look stunning," she says, her eyes twinkling with genuine admiration.

She is in her mid-forties, with auburn hair pulled back into a neat bun and a stylish, yet professional, outfit that compliments her figure. She moves gracefully, her presence calming as she adjusts the dress, ensuring it fits perfectly.

"Thank you," I murmur, still in awe of my reflection. "I've never worn anything like this before."

Laura chuckles softly. "Most brides haven't. This is your special day, after all. You want it to look perfect."

As she works, I can't help but ask, "Do you know Marcus well?"

Her hands pause for a moment, then resume their gentle adjustments. "Only what I've heard. He's a good man, despite what some people might tell you. He's done a lot for this community."

I raise an eyebrow, skeptical. "Really?"

Laura nods, her eyes meeting mine in the mirror. "Oh yes. He helps all the businesses in the area, does favors for anyone who asks, and never denies a request.

"Last month, Mary who ran the bookstore on Third, she passed away. They were going to put her cat down, but Marcus took it in. He paid for her funeral and bought out the mortgage on the store so the staff could all keep their jobs. I heard it all from this girl who works there."

I blink, taken aback. This isn't the ruthless mafia boss I thought I knew. "But... he's a criminal, isn't he?"

"Define criminal." She finishes her adjustments and steps back, admiring her work. "Life isn't always black and white, dear. Marcus has his ways with those who cross him, but he also has a heart, I'm sure. He's getting through life the best he can, just like everyone else."

She pats my shoulder reassuringly. "Now, let's go out and see how you look in the big mirrors."

I step out of the changing room with Laura by my side, feeling a bit more confident. But as we enter the main area of the boutique, my heart stops.

Marcus's bodyguards are slumped against the wall, their eyes vacant and lifeless. Blood seeps into the polished floor, forming dark, sinister pools.

Sitting between the corpses is a man I don't recognize. He is in his fifties, white, and slightly overweight, his body pressing against the tailored lines of his expensive charcoal suit.

His thinning hair is slicked back with meticulous care, and a polite smile plays at his lips, at odds with the brutality he's wrought. His eyes, a cold and calculating blue, flicker with a hidden malevolence beneath the veneer of civility.

"Such heartwarming things to hear about Marcus Rossi," he says, his voice smooth and courteous, as if greeting us in a drawing room rather than a murder scene.

Laura starts screaming, her hand flying to her mouth as she stares at the carnage, unable to reconcile the polite man with the horror around him.

"Sit over there and say nothing," the man orders her, his voice cold and authoritative, waving her away. "I'm not here for you. Relax."

Laura nods quickly, her face pale, and moves to the corner of the room. My heart pounds in my chest as I take in the scene, fear gripping me. The man's eyes meet mine, and he smiles chillingly.

"Hello, Kelsey," he says smoothly. "We need to talk about you and your husband to be. Take a seat."

I swallow hard, trying to keep my voice steady. "Who are you?"

He brushes invisible dust from his suit. "I'm someone who has a vested interest in your future. Sit down."

I glance at Laura, who nods frantically, silently urging me to comply. I sit down, my heart racing.

"Let's make this simple," he begins, his tone deceptively calm. "You're going to do exactly as I say, or things will get very unpleasant for you and everyone you care about, starting with her over there."

The weight of my situation settles heavily on my shoulders. I glance down at the beautiful dress, feeling trapped in a nightmare I can't escape. The luxurious setting, the delicate lace, and satin, all seem like a cruel joke now.

With my father, the violence was signposted, his face dark, his veins bulging. This man, I feel, would kill me without his face changing expression.

"Who are you?" I ask, my voice barely a whisper, my throat dry with fear.

"My name is Rafael Hawke." He regards me coolly, his eyes assessing. "Your father came to see me after Marcus kidnapped you. Asked me to help. Mentioned he's part of my family, a distant associate but I take care of my own."

He reaches into his coat and pulls out a small vial. "This is untraceable. Simply put it in Marcus's food or drink, and it will look like he died of heart failure. You'll be free."

I stare at the vial, my mind racing. The promise of freedom dangles in front of me, but the reality of what he's asking me to do is terrifying. My hands shake as I take the vial from him, feeling its cold weight in my palm.

"What do you stand to gain from Marcus's death?" I ask.

"Clever girl, I see why he likes you." He is still holding the vial toward me. "Take it. Don't make me shoot her to make my point."

I reach out and take it from him, gripping it in my palm. "You want me to kill Marcus. I deserve to know why."

"I would kill him myself but it would lead to war between the two families. That's bad for business. This way, he's gone, and I rule over the city. You get your freedom, and a million dollars each for you and your father. How does that sound?

"One catch, you must be married first."

I nod. "So I inherit all his money when he dies. Let me guess, you take it from me?"

"Like I said, smart girl. You get a million. That's plenty for street scum like you. All you have to do is get rid of a cockroach. Now, off you go. I want to have words with your friend here."

"She's nothing to do with this, leave her alone."

He pulls out a gun, pointing it at her. "You walk out of here, Kelsey, or her brains ruin those pretty dresses behind her. Your choice."

I glance outside, seeing a cop through the window. "Fine," I say, running for the door. "I'm going." I mouth silently toward Laura, "Cop outside. Hold on."

I run for the door, tugging the cop's shoulder as he walks by.

I stumble, nearly tripping over the hem of the dress, my breath coming in short, panicked gasps. Desperation fuels my movements as I grab onto him, my eyes wide with fear.

"Please, help me!" I beg, clutching his arm. "There's two dead men in there."

He looks at me, his eyes narrowing as he takes in my panicked appearance. "Calm down, miss. What happened?" he asks, his voice cautious but concerned.

"Rafael Hawkes' in there. He's killed two people and taken the owner hostage. You have to do something. I think he's about to do something to her. He's got a gun."

"If I were you, Kelsey," the cop says. "I'd do what Don Hawke tells you. Do us all a favor and kill Marcus Rossi."

The door to the store bursts open and Laura springs out, sprinting off down the street, her top ripped down the middle. Hawke emerges, waving her goodbye. "Slippery one," he says, "Got out of my grip." He turns to the cop. "Andrew, good to see you. Any trouble out here?"

"None at all. Kelsey was just going, weren't you?"

He waves down a cab, pulling the door open. "Get in."

Behind him, Rafael smiles coldly at me. "Do the right thing," he says.

I climb inside the cab, pushing the hem of the dress so it fits through the doorway. He calls out to the cabbie. "Take her to the church on Seventeenth. Her fiancé will be there."

━━

I STUMBLE out of the cab, my mind racing. Marcus's at the top of the steps, talking to the priest. "Couldn't wait any longer?" he asks, nodding toward the wedding dress.

"Marcus, your bodyguards... they're dead. There was a man in the shop," I blurt out, panic clear in my voice. "Rafael Hawke."

Marcus curses under his breath, glancing at his watch. His jaw tightens, and he grabs my arm. "What did he say?"

I think of the vial, tucked into my bra. Should I tell him or not? "He said I was under his protection, me and my father. Part of his family."

"I bet he did. Tony and Alex dead. Fuck, we need to move fast." He looks from me to the priest. "We're getting married. Now."

"What? Why?"

He pulls me closer, his grip firm but not painful. "Because that will give you my name as protection. If he sends anyone to hurt you, they will die quickly and painfully. He dare not touch you once you have my name. There are rules between the families. Marriage is sacred. Lucky, you're already in the right dress." He pulls me through the door. "Let's do this."

"No, listen, don't marry me, please. You don't understand."

He glares at me, lowering his voice. The next words out of your mouth will be 'I do' or you'll see my bad side. This is to protect you. Now, get in there."

NINE

Kelsey
───────────

Inside, the church is quiet, the air thick with incense. The vicar scurries toward us. "Don Rossi, I thought today was about touring the venue. Why's she in a wedding dress?"

"Marry us," Marcus demands, his voice brooking no argument. "No questions. Get it done."

The priest's eyes widen in confusion and fear. "But there are rules," he says, his voice trembling. "You have to do it the right way."

Marcus's eyes narrow. "You want to die?" he asks, pulling out a gun and aiming it at the priest. "You sort the fucking paperwork later. Do it."

He reaches into his pocket and pulls out a small velvet box. My heart skips a beat as he opens it to reveal two rings, one delicate and adorned with diamonds, the other a simple, masculine band.

"I had these made for us," he says, his voice steady and unwavering.

I stare at the rings, my mind reeling. "You had these made? How fast do you work?"

"People work hard when you pay as well as I do," he replies smoothly.

"But he killed your men," I protest, trying to muster some defiance in the face of his overwhelming presence. "Don't you care?"

His expression hardens, his eyes narrowing. "I'll deal with that later."

"I can't just marry you like this," I argue, desperation creeping into my voice. "He said he wanted us to get married. You do this and you're playing his game."

His grip on my arm tightens, his gaze turning cold. "Lies. If you continue to argue, I'll pull your panties down and spank you right here, order your father killed, and then marry you anyway. Do you understand?"

I wonder how I could ever have found him appealing. He's nothing but the devil, an animal without human emotion. The vial hidden in my bra feels suddenly like a good idea.

Humiliation washes over me, my cheeks burning with shame as I think of him spanking me. Then I think of my father dead. I glance away, unable to meet his eyes. "Fine," I whisper, my voice barely audible. "I'll do it but I fucking hate you."

"Most people do," he says, his tone softening slightly. "Now, let's get this over with."

The priest stands nervously, wringing his hands. The man looks terrified, his eyes darting around the church as if searching for an escape. Marcus gestures impatiently for him to begin, and the man stammers out the opening words of the ceremony.

"Dearly beloved, we are gathered here today..."

I stand beside Marcus, my heart pounding in my chest. I can feel his presence beside me, commanding and overpowering. "Get to the 'I do's.'"

The priest's voice wavers, his fear palpable, but he continues, his gaze flicking nervously between us.

"Do you, Marcus Rossi, take this woman, Kelsey Dawson, to be your lawfully wedded wife?"

"I do," Marcus replies without hesitation, his voice firm and confident.

The priest turns to me, his eyes filled with a mixture of pity and fear. "And do you, Kelsey, take this man, to be your lawfully wedded husband?"

I swallow hard, my throat dry. "I do," I manage to say.

"By the power vested in me, I now pronounce you husband and wife," the priest concludes, his relief evident.

Marcus slips the delicate ring onto my finger, his touch possessive and final. I slide the simple band onto his finger, my hands trembling.

The priest steps back, his face pale. "You may kiss the bride," he says, his voice shaking.

Marcus doesn't hesitate. His hands grip my waist firmly, yet there's a gentleness to his touch that sends shivers down my spine. Our eyes lock for a fleeting moment, and then his lips are on mine, capturing them in a kiss that is both demanding and intoxicating.

His lips are surprisingly soft yet unyielding, moving against mine with a confidence that leaves no room for doubt. It's a kiss that speaks of possession, of claiming me as his own.

My initial resistance melts away as the heat of his kiss sears through me, igniting a fire I didn't know existed.

His tongue lightly brushes against my lips, coaxing them to part, and when they do, he deepens the kiss, his tongue exploring my mouth with a thoroughness that makes my knees weak.

The intensity of the kiss overwhelms me. Every nerve ending in my body comes alive, sparking with an electrifying mix of fear and desire. I feel his breath mingling with mine.

His hands move up to cradle my face, fingers threading through my hair, holding me in place as if he never wants to let go.

I'm acutely aware of every sensation. The warmth of his body pressed against mine, the faint taste of mint on his lips, the way his stubble lightly grazes my skin.

It's the first kiss I've ever experienced, a kiss that makes me feel possessed and cherished all at once. I'm lost in it, drowning in the waves of emotion that crash over me— lust, vulnerability, and an unsettling sense of belonging.

My hands find their way to his chest, feeling the hard muscles beneath his shirt. I want to push him away and pull him closer all at once. The conflict tears at me, but the desire burning inside is stronger. I press against him, responding to the kiss with a fervor that surprises even me.

Marcus's kiss turns more demanding, his tongue exploring

every corner of my mouth, staking his claim. I moan softly, the sound swallowed by his lips.

His hands slide down my back, pulling me even closer until there's no space left between us. The kiss is relentless, consuming, and it leaves me breathless, my heart pounding in my chest.

When he finally pulls away, it's as if the air has been sucked out of the room. I'm left standing there, dazed and breathless, my lips tingling from the intensity of our kiss.

My heart races, my body trembling from the aftershocks of the passion we just shared. I can see the raw desire in his eyes, a reflection of my own tumultuous feelings.

Marcus's gaze softens, though the possessiveness remains. "You're mine now, Kelsey. Remember that."

I nod, unable to find the words to respond. The kiss has left me feeling more alive and turned on than I've ever been, but also more scared.

The power Marcus holds over me is undeniable, and the kiss was a stark reminder of that. Yet, amidst the fear, there's a part of me that craves more. More of his touch, more of his kiss, more of the man who can make me feel so much with just one kiss.

The priest clears his throat nervously. "Congratulations," he says, his voice wavering. "I'll sign to say the witnesses were here. It'll all be legal, I swear."

Marcus nods, a satisfied smile playing on his lips. "Remember, Kelsey," he says, his voice low and commanding. "You're mine now. And I take care of what's mine."

As we leave the church, Marcus's grip on my hand is unyielding. "You're now safe," he continues, his voice low and intense. "Rafael Hawke thinks by stealing from me, he'll rile me. Killed Tony and Alex to nudge me into over-reacting, making a mistake, give him a chance to end me. I won't play his games. I'll do this my way." He glances across the street. "Over here."

He leads me over to a huge bookstore. Rows upon rows of books greet me as I step inside, the scent of paper and ink calming my frazzled nerves.

"Get anything you want," he says, handing me a credit card. "It has no limit. Use it to keep yourself happy and help with your future studies. Call it a wedding gift. I need to make some calls."

I stare at the card, disbelief mingling with a strange sense of gratitude. "Why are you doing this?" I ask, my voice tinged with suspicion.

Marcus shrugs, his expression unreadable. "Consider it an investment in your future. My wife should be well-educated. Just don't wander too far."

"What did my father steal? What's so important to you?"

"A necklace that belonged to my grandmother. I will get it back. Hawke will die. That's as certain as the sun setting each day. Now go shopping, I've got calls to make."

I nod slowly, taking the credit card and wandering through the aisles. The freedom to choose anything feels surreal. I start picking out medical books and novels that catch my eye, trying to distract myself from the thought that I'm married to a monster.

As I browse, I notice Marcus making calls over by the window, his voice inaudible.

As I look, I find myself thinking of the vial of poison. The weight of the decision I need to make presses down on me. Should I use it? Kill my husband or let him live? Earn a million or remain with a monster?

He reappears in front of me, glancing at the pile of books in my arms. "Make it snappy," he says. "We're due at the opera in thirty minutes."

TEN

Kelsey
___

The lights dim as we settle into the private box at the opera house. I glance around, my eyes wide, taking in the opulence.

Marcus bought me a new outfit on the way here and two more silent bodyguards stand outside our box. It's like Tony and Alex never existed.

Velvet curtains, gilded decorations, and the faint scent of expensive perfume fill the air. Marcus sits beside me, his presence commanding and magnetic. I sip my drink, trying to calm my nerves.

"Why are we here?" I ask.

His eyes glint in the dim light as he leans closer. "Just enjoy the music, Kelsey."

"This isn't a scene in Pretty Woman," I mutter, half to myself. "And you're no Richard Gere. I don't remember him threatening to kill anyone."

He raises an eyebrow. "Pretty Woman? What's that?"

I can't help but chuckle, shaking my head. "It's a movie. How have you not heard of it? It's a classic."

He smirks. "Consider this a cultural exchange. Tonight we watch Faust. Tomorrow night, we'll watch your movie."

His touch sends shivers down my spine, a mix of fear and excitement swirling inside me. The way he looks at me, with such intensity, makes it hard to breathe.

I feel his hand move to my leg, his fingers grazing my thigh through the thin fabric of my dress. The sexual tension between us is palpable, almost suffocating.

His eyes narrow as he looks out into the audience. "I'll be back shortly," he says, his voice low and dangerous.

Before I can respond, he's gone. I watch in stunned silence as he appears down in the audience, grabbing a man who just sat down on the back row, dragging him backward through the doors before anyone notices.

I try to gather my thoughts, my heart still racing from the intensity of our encounter. The opera begins, but my mind is elsewhere, caught between the fear of what Marcus is capable of and the undeniable attraction I feel towards him.

Who was that down there? What's happening? Is that why we're here, because he needed to find that man? Am I just an accessory to his life, to be discarded when he needs to get work done? Would he be as indifferent to my death as to his bodyguards?

Marcus returns a few minutes later, his expression calm and composed as if nothing happened. He sits back down beside me, his hand finding its way back to my leg. "Did you miss me?" he asks, a hint of a smile playing on his lips.

I roll my eyes, trying to mask the fluttering in my stomach. "Who was that?" I ask, keeping my voice steady. "The guy you dragged out of there."

"Just someone I needed to speak to," he replies nonchalantly.

"Did you kill him?" I ask, half-joking, half-serious.

"It might surprise you to know I don't murder everyone I speak to," he says, a playful glint in his eye. His fingers slide up my thigh, sending a jolt of electricity through me.

"Don't you?" My breath catches as he strokes my skin, the touch both soothing and maddening.

"Enjoying the show?" he murmurs, his voice low and intimate.

"I was, until you decided to play gangster," I retort, trying to ignore the heat pooling between my legs.

He chuckles softly, his breath warm against my ear. "You know, you're cute when you try to act tough."

"I'm not acting," I snap, though my voice lacks conviction. His hand continues its slow journey, inching higher up my thigh, making it hard to think straight. "I just don't want to be involved in whatever... this is."

"Too late for that," he says, his fingers tracing patterns on my skin. "You're already involved. Deeply involved. You know what Faust is about?"

I squirm in my seat, the sensation of his touch both thrilling and terrifying. "Marcus, stop it," I whisper, though there's a part of me that doesn't want him to.

"A man sells his soul to the devil in return for everything his heart desires. Remind you of anything?" His voice is teasing, but there's a dangerous edge to it. "Not scared of the devil, are you?"

"Yes," I admit, my heart pounding in my chest. "Terrified."

"Good," he says, his hand slipping further up, brushing against the edge of my panties. "Makes you feel alive, doesn't it? First time I had a gun to my head was like ice water to my face. It woke me up. I've been awake ever since.

"Bastard tried to rob me when I was walking home from school, had no idea who I was. My father found him, let me beat him to death. Once you've watched the lights fade from someone's eyes, you change, Kelsey. Like Faust. You made a deal with the devil."

His touch sends a shiver down my spine, and I bite my lip to keep from moaning. The opera plays on, but I can't focus on anything other than Marcus's fingers, which are now teasing the sensitive skin at the apex of my thighs.

"Marcus, please," I beg, though I'm not sure if I'm asking him to stop or to continue.

"Please, what?" he asks, his voice a seductive whisper.

I struggle to find the words, my mind a haze of desire and confusion. "Please, don't do this," I finally manage to say.

He leans in closer, his lips brushing against my ear. "Why not? Don't you like it?"

"I do, but—"

"No buts," he interrupts, his fingers slipping beneath the fabric of my panties. "I heard you call my name when you came. I know you want this. Stop fighting it. Just feel."

A gasp escapes my lips as his fingers find my clit, stroking gently at first, then with increasing intensity. He heard me last night? Was I that loud?

My body responds to his touch, my hips arching involuntarily. "See? I told you you'd enjoy it," he murmurs, his lips grazing my ear as he whispers.

The pleasure builds slowly, a delicious ache that spreads through my entire body. I try to focus on the stage, but it's impossible. Every stroke of his fingers sends waves of sensation rippling through me, making it harder to breathe, to think.

"Marcus," I moan softly, my hands gripping the armrest of my seat. "Someone might see."

"No one's paying attention," he reassures me, his voice a dark promise. "Just relax and enjoy it."

I close my eyes, letting the sensations wash over me. His fingers move expertly, coaxing me closer and closer to the edge. My mind is a whirlwind of emotions—fear, desire, shame, and an overwhelming need for release.

"Tell me you want this," he demands, his voice rough with need.

"No, I can't."

"I won't let you come unless you tell me."

I try to keep silent but his touch is unraveling all my defenses. "I... I want this," I confess, my voice trembling.

"Good girl," he praises, his fingers moving faster, pushing me towards the brink.

The tension builds, coiling tight in my belly until I can't hold back any longer. With a muffled cry, I come undone, my body shuddering with the force of my orgasm. The singing on stage covers the gasps escaping my mouth but only just.

His fingers continue their relentless rhythm, drawing out every last bit of pleasure until I'm a trembling, breathless mess.

As the waves of pleasure subside, I open my eyes to find him watching me, his expression a mixture of satisfaction and possessiveness. He withdraws his hand from my panties, licking his fingers with a smug grin.

"You look beautiful when you come," he says, his voice low and intimate. He leans over and kisses my cheek. "Next time it won't be my hand that makes you come."

ELEVEN

Kelsey

The moment we step into Marcus's penthouse, the air changes. The opulence and grandeur are still here, but the atmosphere is charged with a tension that wasn't present when I left.

Marcus closes the door behind us and turns to face me, his gaze intense and unwavering.

"We're now man and wife," he declares, his voice low and commanding. "And I'm going to fuck you until you get pregnant."

My heart skips a beat at his bluntness. The reality of the situation crashes over me, but I manage to find my voice. "I'm a virgin," I admit, my voice barely above a whisper. "I've never done this before."

A predatory smile spreads across his face. "I guessed that already," he says, stepping closer. "I'll be your first and your only."

"Can we at least have the lights out?" I ask, hoping to soften the impact of what's about to happen.

He nods, a rare gesture of accommodation. "If that makes you more comfortable."

He flips the switch, plunging the room into darkness. I take my chance and tuck the vial under the couch cushions.

I hear his footsteps approaching, slow and deliberate. My heart pounds in my chest as I wait for his next move. Did he notice what I did?

Then, I feel his lips on mine. The kiss is deep and consuming, igniting a fire within me that I didn't know existed. I melt into him, my body responding instinctively to his touch. He breaks the kiss, and I'm left gasping for air, my lips tingling from the intensity.

"You're mine, Kelsey," he murmurs against my lips, his breath hot and tantalizing. "I'm going to come inside your pussy over and over again until you're pregnant."

His hands roam over my body, exploring every curve. One hand finds its way between my legs, his fingers slipping under my panties. I gasp at the sensation, my body tensing in anticipation.

He moves his fingers expertly, drawing out pleasure with every stroke.

"Relax," he whispers, his voice a mixture of command and coaxing.

I try to comply, but my mind is a whirlwind of conflicting emotions. His touch is both thrilling and terrifying, and I'm torn between the urge to push him away and the desire to pull him closer.

His fingers work their magic, bringing me closer to the edge. My breaths come in shallow gasps, and I can feel the tension building within me.

Despite my attempts to resist, my body betrays me, responding eagerly to his touch.

"Good girl," he murmurs, his voice a dark promise.

I moan softly as he continues his ministrations, each movement pushing me closer to release. My legs tremble, and I clutch at his shoulders for support, my nails digging into his skin.

"Let go," he urges, his tone leaving no room for defiance.

With a final, skilled motion, he brings me to orgasm. My body shudders against him, waves of pleasure crashing over me. I bite my lip to stifle a cry, overwhelmed by the intensity of the moment.

As I come down from the high, he pulls his fingers away, leaving me feeling both satiated and vulnerable. The darkness surrounds us, but I can feel his presence, powerful and dominant.

His fingers, slick from my arousal, trail up my arm, leaving a path of fire in their wake. I can feel my heart racing, each beat a reminder of the intense pleasure he just gave me.

My mind is a chaotic mix of fear, desire, and confusion. How can something so wrong feel so incredibly right?

"Now," he says, his voice a low rumble in the darkness, "I'm going to push your boundaries further."

I'm about to protest, to find some semblance of control in this situation, but he silences me with another searing kiss.

His lips are demanding, commanding my complete surrender. And I give it, melting into him once again.

His hands move to the hem of my dress, lifting it over my head and tossing it aside. The cool air hits my bare skin, and I shiver, a mixture of excitement and apprehension.

His touch is everywhere, exploring, claiming. His hands are rough yet skilled, knowing exactly where to press and tease to elicit the most delicious reactions from me. My bra is unhooked, flung away from me.

He steps back for a moment, and I hear the rustle of fabric. When he returns, his skin is hot against mine.

He's removed his shirt, and the feel of his bare chest against my breasts sends another wave of desire coursing through me. His skin is warm, his muscles hard and unyielding. Every inch of him exudes power and control. My nipples tingle against his chest.

I feel his hand on my thigh, pushing my legs apart. His touch is firm, insistent. He rips my panties from my body in his impatience.

He's giving me no choice but to comply, to open myself to him completely. And despite the fear gnawing at the edges of my consciousness, I can't help but want it. Want him.

He's rougher now, his touch more demanding. His fingers find my core again, but this time, he doesn't tease. He plunges inside me, his fingers moving with purpose. I gasp, the sensation overwhelming. It's too much, too intense, but I don't want him to stop.

"Tell me you want this," he growls, his voice a dark, seductive command.

I bite my lip, trying to hold back the words. I don't want to give him the satisfaction, but my body betrays me. Every nerve is on fire, every inch of my skin alive with sensation. I can't deny the truth.

"Say it," he demands, his fingers thrusting deeper.

"I want this," I whisper as my pussy aches with emptiness.

"Louder," he commands, his breath hot against my ear.

"I want this," I repeat, louder this time. "I want you in me."

He rewards my compliance with a fierce kiss, his tongue invading my mouth, claiming me completely. The taste of him is intoxicating, a mix of dominance and desire that leaves me breathless.

In the darkness, his hands are everywhere, pushing me to the brink of madness. He lifts me effortlessly, positioning me on the bed. I feel the mattress beneath me, soft and luxurious, a stark contrast to the roughness of his touch.

"Are you ready?" he asks, his voice a tantalizing whisper.

"Yes," I breathe, my body trembling with anticipation.

His weight presses down on me, a comforting and terrifying presence all at once. His lips find my neck, trailing kisses down to my collarbone, his breath hot against my skin. I arch into him, my body aching for more.

He takes his time, savoring every inch of me. His mouth moves lower, his tongue tracing patterns over my breasts, sending shivers down my spine. I'm lost in the sensation, in the way he makes me feel.

His hand moves between my legs again, spreading me open for him. He positions himself at my entrance, and I can feel the tip of his cock pressing against me. It's a moment of pure, raw anticipation.

"This might hurt," he warns, his voice surprisingly gentle.

I nod, bracing myself. He pushes inside, slowly, giving me time to adjust. The pain is sharp at first, a stark contrast to the pleasure that follows. He fills me completely, stretching me in a way that's both uncomfortable and exhilarating.

"Relax," he murmurs, his lips brushing against mine.

I try to follow his advice, focusing on the feel of him inside me. He moves slowly at first, each thrust deliberate and controlled.

The pain begins to fade, replaced by a growing pleasure. I can feel every inch of him, the way he fills me, the way he claims me.

"Good girl," he whispers, his voice filled with approval.

His pace quickens, and the pleasure intensifies. I moan, unable to hold back the sounds of my desire. He's everywhere, surrounding me, overwhelming me.

Each thrust sends waves of pleasure through me, building to an inevitable climax.

He groans, a deep, primal sound that sends shivers down my spine. His thrusts become harder, more urgent. I'm on the edge, teetering on the brink of release.

"Come for me," he commands, his voice a dark promise.

And I do. The orgasm crashes over me, powerful and

consuming. My body convulses around him, and I cry out, the pleasure too intense to contain.

He follows me over the edge, his release mingling with mine, filling me completely.

As the waves of pleasure subside, he collapses beside me, pulling me into his arms. We lie there in the darkness, our bodies entwined, our breaths mingling. For a moment, everything is perfect.

"I'll keep doing that until you're pregnant," he whispers, his voice a mix of satisfaction and promise. "I'm going to fuck you every single day until you give me an heir."

I want to hate him for saying those words. But, as he kisses the side of my neck, I can't stop myself smiling.

TWELVE

Kelsey

I sit on the plush couch, flipping through the college brochures in my lap. Barney, the cat, curls up next to me, purring softly.

The brochures are filled with bright, smiling faces and promises of a future that felt impossible just a short time ago.

I stroke Barney absentmindedly, my thoughts a tangled web of guilt, corruption, and an unexpected acceptance of my new life. I glance down at my wedding ring.

I'm his wife. I'm married to a mafia boss. Hidden in my bedroom is vial, carefully retrieved from the couch in the middle of the night. I could kill my husband but do I want to? That's the big question.

I'm no longer a virgin. We didn't just have sex, it was unprotected. I could be pregnant already. The idea is insane but I can't stop myself from smiling. Have I gone totally crazy?

When I woke up this morning Marcus was already gone. More meetings, no doubt. Deciding who to kill today, I'm guessing.

The aroma of breakfast wafts through the air, and I glance towards the kitchen where Chase is busy at the stove.

It's strange having someone cook for me, a stark contrast to the life I've known. Every morning I had to make breakfast for my father, for as long as I can remember. Always wincing, waiting to see what I got wrong today, what pain he would inflict. I look at my bruises. For the first time they're fading without new ones forming.

I feel like a different person, both physically and emotionally. My hair is styled in a way I would never have chosen for myself, and the outfit I'm wearing is revealing and elegant, making me feel both exposed and empowered.

Despite the turmoil inside me, I find myself starting to accept this new role and the luxury that comes with it. I can't help but think about last night over and over.

The memory of Marcus's touch, his intensity, the way he made me feel—it all floods back, evoking a mix of emotions. I feel trapped by his need and possessiveness, yet there's an undeniable intrigue that pulls at me.

I take a deep breath, resolving not to let Marcus break me. There's strength to be found in this situation, and I'm determined to grasp it.

My thoughts drift again to the possibility of getting pregnant, the bond it would create between Marcus and me. The idea fills me with both terror and a strange sense of joy. What would it be like to carry his child, to have a part of him growing inside me?

As I imagine the future, I begin to accept the strange calm that Marcus has brought into my life. I don't know what kind of parents we would be, but there's a bizarre comfort in the uncertainty. The chaos feels almost natural now, a new normal that I'm slowly embracing.

Chase sets a plate of breakfast in front of me, and I thank him quietly. He nods and retreats, leaving me alone with my thoughts. I take a bite of the eggs, savoring the rich, delicate flavor. It's the best meal I've had in a long time.

I drop a piece of egg to Barney, who devours it eagerly, his tail flicking with contentment.

Marcus appears from the elevator, joining me at the table, his presence commanding as always. He pours himself a cup of coffee. "Did you sleep well?" he asks, his voice a mix of casual concern and authority.

"Well enough," I reply, trying to keep my tone neutral. Did he see me retrieve the vial? Is this a test?

"There's a meeting later today," he continues, taking a sip of his coffee. "I want you there."

I look at him, surprised. "Why do you want me at one of your meetings?"

"I want you to see what I do, understand my world. It's important."

I nod slowly, feeling a mix of relief and anxiety. "Do I have a choice?"

"Let's put it this way. I won't be happy if you refuse to attend."

"So I don't have a choice."

"I picked up a copy of Pretty Woman," he continues as if I hadn't spoken. "Ready for our cultural exchange to continue?"

He shows me the box, and despite myself, I can't help but smile. "You won't like it," I tell him.

"Let's see, shall we."

He leads me to yet another room in the penthouse, laid out like a cinema with two boxes of popcorn set next to a pair of reclining chairs.

I settle in beside him as he loads the disc. "Want to know what it's about?" I ask as Barney leaps onto my lap and curls up in a tiny ball.

"A woman who's not unattractive, I'm guessing," he replies with a grin as he looks at the cover. "Just spitballing here."

"You could be a cop with those deductive skills."

"I'm guessing she gets a happy ending too."

"You'll have to see, won't you?"

The movie begins, and within minutes, I find myself relaxing. I know it so well I could recite the entire script for him. What makes me smile isn't the movie, it's seeing him enjoy it for the first time.

He watches in silence, laughing at the jokes like we've been doing this kind of thing for years. His hand finds mine during the polo scene, and my heart starts to race.

By the climax, I'm holding my breath, and even he's sitting more upright. When Richard Gere rocks up through the sunroof, he's laughing, and so am I. A minute later, the credits roll, and he turns to me. "I see why you like it."

"Not as classy as Faust," I reply. "I'll accept that."

"Better," he says. "Less preachy."

"You know, the original ending had him dumping her."

"I see why they changed it. No one wants to see real life on screen. There's enough shit in the world out there, you don't need it in your movie choices."

"My thoughts exactly."

He glances at the time. "I've got some work to do. You picked a college yet?"

"Not yet, still looking."

"Soon as you do, let me know and we'll send them a massive bribe to make sure they accept you."

I roll my eyes. "You can't just solve everything with money, Marcus."

"Why not? It's worked pretty well for me so far."

"You're impossible." I stand up, trying to shake off the strange mix of annoyance and attraction that always simmers between us.

He smirks, leaning back in his chair. "You know, you're really cute when you're mad."

"Don't patronize me," I snap, though I can't help the blush creeping up my cheeks.

"It's not patronizing, it's an observation." He stands up and steps closer, his presence overwhelming. "You're passionate. I like that about you. Now you're out from under your father's shadow, you can be truly passionate."

"Passionate? I'm furious with you half the time."

"Anger can be passion. Two sides of the same coin."

"You think you know everything, don't you?"

"I know enough." His voice drops, and there's a glint in his eyes that sends a shiver down my spine. "I know you're attracted to me."

"Stop it," I whisper, taking a step back.

"Stop what?" He follows, his hand reaching out to tuck a stray strand of hair behind my ear. "Telling the truth?"

"You're insufferable," I say, but my voice lacks conviction.

"Maybe," he admits, his thumb grazing my cheek. "But you can't deny this thing between us."

"There's nothing between us," I lie, my breath hitching as he leans closer.

"Liar," he murmurs before his lips capture mine.

The kiss is explosive, a clash of wills and desires. It's a battle, each of us trying to take control. His hands grip my waist, pulling me closer as I press against him, fists clenched in his shirt.

I hate how good he is at this, how easily he can make me forget everything else. My mind is a whirlwind of confusion, anger, and undeniable attraction.

When he finally pulls away, I'm left breathless, my heart racing. "Damn you," I whisper, hating how much I want him.

He smirks, brushing his thumb over my swollen lips. "Admit it, Kelsey. You feel this too."

"I... I don't know what I feel," I say, my voice shaky. "This is all new to me."

"Then let me show you." His lips find mine again, and this time, I don't resist.

THIRTEEN

Marcus

"A bowling alley?" Kelsey asks. "This is where you have your big mafia meetings?"

She stands beside one of the lanes, looking both amused and skeptical. "What is it, pick up the spare or get a bullet through the head?"

"Pretty much. We've time for a game if you play?"

She laughs, the sound light and infectious. "Don't expect me to go easy on you."

As we lace up our bowling shoes, the atmosphere lightens, the tension between us easing into something more playful. I can't help but notice how radiant she looks, her eyes sparkling with excitement. Her laughter fills the air, a stark contrast to the serious tone that usually surrounds us.

"You sure you can handle the competition?" I tease, handing her a ball. The weight of it is nothing compared to the weight of the moment between us.

"Bring it on," she replies, her voice filled with determination. Her confidence is alluring, a challenge I'm more than ready to accept.

With surprising skill, she swings the ball back and releases it with perfect form. It glides smoothly down the lane, crashing into the pins with a satisfying thud. "Strike!" she exclaims, turning to face me, her eyes sparkling with triumph.

"Impressive," I admit, grabbing my own ball. "But don't get too cocky."

As I line up my shot, she moves closer, watching me intently. "You know, my dad used to get furious whenever I won at anything," she says, her tone light but with an edge of bitterness. "He couldn't stand the idea of me being better than him at something. Except bowling. It was the only thing he wanted me to learn to be good at. God knows why."

"Sounds like a real charmer," I reply as she nudges my arm, sending my ball careering to the left into the gutter. "Some might call that cheating."

She laughs, the sound light and musical. "Guess you'll have to try harder. Or are you afraid of being shown up by a girl?"

I step back, watching as she prepares for her next turn. "I didn't come here to lose," I say, grinning. "But I have to admit, watching you bowl is almost worth it."

She rolls her eyes, but I can see the blush creeping up her cheeks. "Flattery will get you nowhere, Marcus," she teases, sending another perfect strike down the lane, the sight of her ass making my cock twitch. "Your turn."

As the game progresses, she seems to relax into herself, her eyes lighting up with genuine joy. "You've got some serious skills," I say, genuinely impressed.

"Don't underestimate me," she replies, her voice low and playful. "I might just surprise you."

She smirks, her confidence growing with each successful throw.

"Maybe you should take a few pointers from me," she suggests, her eyes twinkling with mischief.

"Maybe I will," I say, feeling the electric charge between us. "But for now, I think it's time to up the stakes."

"Oh?" she asks, raising an eyebrow. "What do you have in mind?"

I take a step closer, our faces inches apart. "If I win, you have to do something for me. Something I choose."

"And if I win?" she counters, her breath warm against my skin.

"Then I'll do something for you. Anything you want."

She bites her lip, considering the offer. "Deal. But don't be too disappointed when I win."

The game continues, the playful teasing mixed with the growing tension between us. Each strike, each spare, each near miss brings us closer together. The stakes are high, but the connection between us is even higher.

As the game draws to a close, it's clear she's got the upper hand. I deliberately miss a few shots, wanting to see her win, to see that triumphant look on her face.

"Looks like I win," she announces, her voice filled with satisfaction. "So, about my prize."

I step closer, my eyes locked onto hers. "How about this?" I say, pulling her into a kiss. It's electric, a spark that ignites something deep within me, something I hadn't expected. "Double or nothing. I win, I give you an orgasm right here."

"And if I win?"

"I let you go. Still pay for your medical training into the bargain."

The kiss deepens, our bodies pressed close together. When we finally pull apart, we're both breathless, our hearts racing. "You know," I add, my lips brushing against hers, "you're really something else, Kelsey."

"Feeling's mutual," she replies, her voice husky. "But don't think this means you can let me win every time."

I laugh, pulling her closer. "I wouldn't dream of it. But right now, I think we've got more important things to focus on."

"Like this?" she asks, though the glint in her eyes tells me she's got something planned.

On her next turn, she leans forward further than normal, her skirt lifting just enough to give me a tantalizing glimpse of her panties. My protective instincts flare, mingling with a rush of desire. It's a combination that leaves me slightly off-balance, a rare feeling for me.

"Careful there," I say, my voice low and teasing as she stands back up. "You wouldn't want to distract me too much."

"Oh, I'm counting on it," she retorts, a playful smirk on her lips. "Anything to throw you off your game."

I step up for my turn, feeling her eyes on me. The pressure is on, but I thrive under it. I line up my shot and send the ball down the lane, knocking over all but one pin.

"Close, but not quite," she says, her laughter infectious. "Looks like you're losing your touch."

"Just you wait," I reply, retrieving the ball. "The night's still young."

The game becomes even more intense, each of us focused on winning. Her competitive spirit is intoxicating, matching my own in a way I hadn't expected. On one of her turns, she leans over again, and this time, I can't help but stare at her ass.

"Enjoying the view?" she calls back, catching me in the act.

"Very much," I admit, unabashed. "But don't think that's going to distract me. I was just checking your form."

"Is that what you call it?" She smirks, clearly pleased with herself.

As the game draws to a close, it's clear she's got the upper hand. I deliberately miss a few shots, wondering if I want to see her win. The triumphant look on her face is almost worth it.

"You need three strikes in a row," she says, glancing up at the scoreboard. "Good luck with that."

"You know, I used to come here every single night after work," I say, firing down the center for a strike. "Look at that. There's one."

"Two more to go," she says, standing to one side of the lane.

As I stride forward, she flashes her panties at me with a grin.

I ignore her, getting another strike. "One rule in my life," I say, collecting another ball.

"Never get distracted." I roll it forward again, hitting the final strike I need.

"Looks like I win," I say. "Come with me."

I take her hand, leading her to the bathroom. The anticipation between us is electric, every step heightening the tension.

Inside, I push her against the wall, my fingers finding their way between her legs.

"Marcus," she breathes, her voice a mix of anticipation and desire.

I don't waste any time, my fingers moving expertly, drawing out soft moans from her. Her body responds eagerly, hips moving in time with my motions. I can feel her getting closer, her breaths coming in shallow gasps.

"Marcus," she whispers, her voice trembling with need. "Please."

"Please what?" I tease, my lips grazing her earlobe. "Tell me what you want, Kelsey."

"I want to come," she breathes, her hands gripping my shoulders for support. "I want you to make me come."

I smile against her skin, my fingers slowing their rhythm just enough to drive her wild. "I want to see you swollen with my child, Kelsey. Your belly round and your breasts full. Do you know how much that thought turns me on?"

She moans softly, the sound sending a jolt of desire through me. "Don't stop," she begs.

"I'm not going to stop," I promise, my fingers picking up the pace again. "I want to make you feel so good, Kelsey. I want you to remember this every time you look at me."

Her breaths come faster, her body arching into my touch. "Marcus, I—"

"Let go for me," I murmur, my lips brushing against her ear. "I want to feel you come in my arms. I want to see that look in your eyes when you can't take it anymore."

She shudders, her orgasm washing over her in powerful waves. I hold her steady, my fingers continuing their rhythm until she's completely spent. Watching her come fills me with a sense of possessive satisfaction.

"You're mine, Kelsey," I whisper, my lips trailing kisses along her neck. "Do you understand that? You belong to me."

She nods, her eyes still glazed with pleasure. "Yes, Marcus. I'm yours."

I can't help but smile, my heart swelling with a fierce protectiveness. "Good. Because I'm never letting you go."

She looks up at me, her eyes softening. "I don't want you to."

I kiss her deeply, pouring all my emotions into the kiss. It's not just about the physical connection anymore. It's about everything we've been through together, everything we still have to face. I want her by my side, no matter what.

When we finally pull apart, she's breathless, her cheeks flushed. "That was…"

"Incredible?" I suggest, grinning. "Perfect, the greatest thing ever?"

She laughs, the sound like music to my ears. "It was all right, I guess."

I pull her close, holding her tight. "I meant what I said, Kelsey. I want to see you pregnant with my child. I want to build a life with you, a family."

"Better than bowling, don't you think?" I whisper, kissing her softly.

She laughs breathlessly, still recovering. "Much better."

We emerge from the bathroom, our connection deeper, the bond between us no longer deniable. As we head to the function room for my meeting, I feel a renewed sense of determination. Kelsey is mine, and I'll do whatever it takes to keep her safe.

The function room is filled with my men, the air thick with tension and respect. I stride in, Kelsey by my side, and the room falls silent.

"Gentlemen," I announce, my voice commanding. "This is my wife, and I expect you to show her the respect she deserves."

They all get to their feet, nodding her way, no one daring to ask how I got married without any of them knowing about it.

Kelsey sits beside me, looking radiant in her outfit, her nervousness tempered by newfound confidence. I find myself captivated by her presence, admiring her strength and beauty.

"You look stunning," I whisper, enjoying the way her smile lights up her face.

"Thank you," she replies, her eyes meeting mine with a mix of gratitude and something deeper.

I stand, drawing the room's attention. "Before we proceed further, there's something you all need to know," I say, my voice cutting through the murmurs. "Kelsey's father stole the necklace that went missing during my 40th birthday party."

The room falls silent, all eyes on Kelsey. She shifts uncomfortably but doesn't break eye contact with me.

I continue, my voice firm. "And now she's part of our family. I expect you to treat her with the same respect you show me."

One of the men, Carlo, steps forward. "Boss, if I may. Isn't her dad connected to the Hawkes?"

"And?"

"Nothing. Just saying."

"Keep your fucking mouth shut if you have nothing useful to say," I reply coldly. "Hawke killed Tony and Alex this morning. He's attempting to antagonize me into acting foolish."

The men exchange looks, a mixture of anger and anticipation in their eyes.

"What's the plan, boss?" Carlo asks, his voice filled with barely contained rage. "Son of bitch needs dealing with, right? Whole family are a bunch of cunts." He looks pointedly at Kelsey.

"We will get our revenge soon enough," I say, my tone icy. "But no one is to act until I give the order. Is that understood?"

A chorus of nods and murmurs of agreement follow. I can feel Kelsey's eyes on me, her gaze a mix of fear and defiance.

Carlo stands up, banging his fist on the table. "Her father stole from you and you don't kill her, but you marry her instead? Then you let Tony and Alex's deaths go unpunished? Did she take your balls from you during the marriage vows?"

As the room settles into a tense silence, I turn to Kelsey. "You see, Kelsey," I say, loud enough for everyone to hear, "in this world, respect is everything. And sometimes, that means taking action to ensure it."

She looks up at me, her eyes wide. "What do you mean?"

I turn to Carlo. "You embarrass me in front of my wife? You question my orders? You infer she's a cunt?"

His eyes widen in fear. "Please, Marcus, I was just saying—"

"Silence," I command, my voice like steel. "You will serve as an example. "Everyone, watch and learn. This is what happens to those who question me."

I walk over to him, the room holding its breath. He glares at me as I stare coldly back at him. "Hand," I say.

"Please," he says, his voice weakening as he realizes what's about to happen. "I misspoke. It won't happen again."

"Damn fucking straight it won't. Hand, now. Don't make me say it again or it'll go off at the wrist."

He sticks his hand out toward me. I grab hold of it and snap two of his fingers, the crunch loud in the room. He winces but manages to avoid crying out.

"Get that seen to," I tell him. "After the meeting." I turn to the rest of my men, my voice cold and commanding. "Let this be a lesson. Questioning me will not be tolerated. Insulting my wife will get you hurt."

I walk back to Kelsey and whisper in her ear, "I want to be in you. Right now."

FOURTEEN

Kelsey

I want to tell him to go to hell when he whispers in my ear, but his voice does things to my body that I can't control. He's just snapped the fingers of one of his own men. I should hate him.

The problem is I see why he did it. To protect my honor.

I've barely had a chance to react to his whispered words when the door bursts open. The cop from outside the wedding boutique is dragged in. He's bleeding and visibly terrified.

"Look what we have here," Marcus says, his voice dripping with disdain. "Andrew, isn't it? I wanted to thank you in person for moving my wedding forward."

The cop's eyes meet mine, pleading. "Please, don't let him kill me," he begs, his voice trembling.

Marcus's gaze hardens. "You helped him kill two of my closest friends," he announces, his tone icy and unforgiving. "You did nothing while he assaulted that poor woman today. You're a disgrace to the uniform. Why should I let you live?"

Andrew's desperation is palpable. "I can help you," he stammers. "I know things about Rafael. I can get you what you want. I can get you the necklace back. That's what all this is about, right?"

Marcus looks at him with a mixture of contempt and curiosity. "And why should I trust you?"

The cop glances at me, hoping for some sympathy. "I can prove it," he insists. "Just give me a chance."

Marcus turns to Carlo. "Your fingers wouldn't be broken if you had more faith in your boss. There's always a plan. Sometimes you just need to wait for the right moment."

Carlo nods back at him, eager to please.

I step forward, trying to project confidence. "Andrew," I say, my voice steady. "You said you can help us. How?"

Marcus looks at me as if he's about to say something but then he falls silent.

Andrew swallows hard, glancing nervously from Marcus to me. "Hawke has a shipment coming in. Drugs, guns, everything. I know where and when. You can hit him where it hurts."

Marcus's eyes narrow. "And why would you betray him so easily?"

"Because you'll kill me if I don't give you something," Andrew admits, desperation creeping into his voice. "I'm no use to him if he finds out I've been here. But I can be useful to you. You can protect me."

Marcus turns to me, his expression unreadable. "Kelsey, what do you think we should do with him?"

The room falls silent, all eyes on me. I take a deep breath, remembering the woman in the wedding boutique, her clothes torn, running for her life. Then I look at the cop, pleading for his life, battered and bruised.

"Maybe he's telling the truth," I reply.

"You trust him? You believe this piece of shit?"

"What harm does it do to listen? Maybe you can get the necklace back without any more bloodshed. That's what you want, isn't it?"

Andrew's face pales. "Please," he pleads. "She's right. I can get it for you. Just spare me. Let me live. I've got a wife, please. Don't kill me."

Marcus looks at him coldly, pulling out a gun and placing it on the table in front of him. "I'll only ask this once. Where is the necklace?"

Andrew looks like he's about to speak.

"Well?"

Out of nowhere, the cop squirms free from the men holding him, hurling himself onto the gun on the table.

He grabs hold of it, pointing it straight at Marcus. "Hawke sends his regards," he says before pulling the trigger.

FIFTEEN

Kelsey

Nothing happens. He frowns down at the gun, clicking the trigger again.

Marcus doesn't blink. An icy cold smile spreads across his lips as he snatches the gun from Andrew's hands. "You think I'm fucking stupid?" he says. "No bullets. Just wanted to see how honest you were. Want to talk again about helping screw over Hawke? Or maybe tell me how he wanted you brought here so you could shoot me."

He turns to me. "Be careful who you trust in future. Desperate people tell lies."

Clenching his fist, he turns, smacking Andrew full in the face, sending him staggering back into the arms of his men. "Hold him," he says. "This is going to be fun."

"Marcus, no!" I shout, my voice barely cutting through the noise as the cop screams for mercy.

Marcus doesn't listen, his fist connecting with Andrew's jaw in another brutal punch that sends him sprawling to the floor. The room falls silent, the sheer force of Marcus's fury stilling everyone. But I see the wild look in my husband's eyes, and I know he's on the edge of going too far as he grabs hold of the gun.

"Please, Marcus, stop!" I beg, stepping forward, my heart pounding.

Marcus pauses, his chest heaving, and for a moment, I think he might ignore me. But then he steps back, lowering his gun. His jaw is set, his eyes still blazing with anger.

"Hold him here," Marcus orders his men, his voice cold and commanding. He turns to me. "This way."

Marcus walks out of the room and over to the bar, ordering two beers before turning to me , his expression hard. "We need to talk," he says. "You can't ever undermine me in front of the men."

"You think that's what I was doing?"

"Telling me to stop hitting him. Pleading for his worthless life."

"I didn't want you to kill him until you'd found out whether or not he knows where your precious necklace is. You were about to kill him. He can't talk if he's dead, can he?"

He looks at me, his eyebrows going up. "I underestimated you. All right, what do I do after he talks?"

"The way I see it, you have two options. Let him go or kill him. You let him go, he could do anything, plus your men think you're weak. We saw that already with Carlo. You kill him, he can't talk, and you maintain your position of power. You've no choice but to kill him."

"Even though he has a wife?"

"He's lying."

"What makes you say that?"

"No wedding ring."

"You're right. I've already checked him out. No wife, no kids, lives alone. Lying through his teeth the whole damn time." He runs a hand through his hair. "In this life, control and security are everything. If we show weakness, we're dead. People exploit weakness."

I take a deep breath, trying to steady myself. "I see that now."

Marcus takes a sip of his beer. "There is no room for emotion when dealing with threats. Pain will make him talk, and we need that information. You might be better off staying out here."

"I'm your wife. Don't you think I belong by your side?"

His eyes narrow, and for a moment, I see the devil everyone fears. "You're potentially going to see a man die."

"We need to be honest with each other. No more secrets."

He takes a deep breath, his eyes locking onto mine. "The man at the opera was Hawke's consigliere. He told me that Hawke gave the necklace to the cop to hide. The cop must have put it somewhere safe. Pain will make him talk."

He drains his drink before getting to his feet. "This way," he says. He heads back into the meeting room, picking up a bowling ball on his way.

I watch him go, my heart heavy with conflicting emotions. I can see the monster he is, but I also see the man who's

trying to protect me, the man who's been hurt and hard-
ened by the darkness around him.

SIXTEEN

Kelsey

I walk back into the meeting room where Andrew is being held. The air is thick with tension. He's tied to a chair, bloodied and bruised. His eyes widen in fear as Marcus steps up to him, setting the bowling ball down on the floor on the way.

"That door is soundproof," Marcus says. "None of the fine guests of this establishment will hear your screams. You're going to tell me where the necklace is."

The cop spits blood at him. Marcus jumps back just in time, smiling as he does so. "Want to play it that way? Fine by me."

He picks up the ball, lifting it high in the air and then letting it fall so it hits Andrew's knee.

The cop screams in agony, his body convulsing in the chair. I flinch, my stomach turning at the sound. I want to look away, but I force myself to keep watching. I need to see this through.

"You want the pain to end?" Marcus says, his voice cold and detached. "Where is the necklace?" He lifts the ball high in the air. "Chance you could still limp out of here when this is over."

The cop's breath comes in ragged gasps. "Okay, okay! Her dad... he knows where it is. Please, just stop!"

"You gave it to Dawson to hide?"

"We did it together. He got fucked for the money and so did I."

"Keep talking."

"The plan was to get you to pay us a couple of mil, then we'd tell you where to find it."

"What about Kelsey? Did he want her back as part of this bargain?" He presses his fist into the cop's injured knee.

"No, fuck, that hurts. He just wants the money, same as me."

"And you don't know where it is?"

"I gave it to Dawson, I swear to God. Go and ask him yourself."

"You know what?" Marcus leans in close to the cop, his voice a deadly whisper. "I believe you."

Before I can process what's happening, Marcus pulls out his silenced gun and shoots Andrew in the head. I gasp, my hand flying to my mouth. I knew this was coming, but the finality of it still shocks me.

Marcus turns to me, his expression softening slightly. "You understand why I did that?"

I swallow hard, looking at the body on the floor. "I understand."

He reaches out, cupping my face in his hands. "You did well."

I look into his eyes, seeing the depth of his pain, the weight of his choices. He's a monster, but there's something more beneath the surface—a damaged man, shaped by his past, trying to find a way to live in a world that demands brutality.

"I'm scared, Marcus," I admit, my voice trembling. "I thought you were the same as my father. But you're different. His violence was senseless, but yours, it has a purpose."

He leans in, his forehead resting against mine. "I do whatever it takes to protect what matters, Kelsey. Whatever it takes."

SEVENTEEN

Kelsey

As we drive to my house, the tension between Marcus and me is palpable. The air is thick with unspoken words and the weight of what we've just done.

I stare out the window, watching the city blur past. Andrew's death lingers in my thoughts, a stark reminder of the darkness that surrounds Marcus's world—and now, by extension, mine.

Marcus's grip on the steering wheel is relaxed. I glance over at him, seeing the calm expression on his face, a mask of control and determination. He notices my gaze and turns to look at me, his eyes hardening slightly.

"You're quiet," he says, breaking the silence.

I take a deep breath, trying to find the right words. "What happened back there. I'm still processing it."

His jaw clenches. "You insisted on being there. This is the reality of my life, Kelsey. Violence, power, control—it's all part of the mafia world. If you want to be involved, you have to accept that."

I nod, swallowing hard. "I know, and I do want to be involved. I feel responsible for his death. He stole the necklace, and now all of this is happening because of it."

Marcus's eyes flicker with something unreadable. "You're not responsible for Hawke's actions. He's the one who decided to play this game. But I understand your guilt. Just know that if you're in, you're all in. There's no turning back."

"I get it," I reply, my voice steady. "But how are we going to get my dad to tell us the truth about the necklace? Does he get tortured too?"

A dark smile tugs at Marcus's lips. "Your dad is a coward. He'll cave under the slightest pressure."

I shiver at his words, a mix of fear and intrigue coursing through me. "And if he doesn't?"

"Then we make him," Marcus says, his tone leaving no room for doubt. "This is my way, Kelsey. Ruthless measures are sometimes the only way to survive."

I look at him, seeing the steel in his eyes, and something inside me shifts. "What about love? Does that come into any of this?"

He's silent for a moment, his expression guarded. But then he sighs, as if deciding to let me in for once. "My mother was the old woman who ran the bookstore. Mary. No one knows but me. My father had countless affairs during his marriage, and I'm the result of one. It was hushed up but he told me the truth when I turned eighteen, told me to keep it quiet or he'd kill her. He taught me that nothing is ever what it seems on the surface."

I reach out and touch his arm, feeling the tension in his muscles. "I'm sorry, Marcus. That's a hard lesson to learn."

He nods, his eyes distant. "It is. And it's made me who I am. My empire is ten times what my father managed. I decided to never let anyone in and it worked, until you."

"This could be different," I say softly. "If you keep your word, if we work together, we can make it something better."

He glances at me, a flicker of hope in his eyes. "Maybe. But you have to understand, Kelsey, this world is filled with death and darkness. You have to accept that to survive."

I nod, determined. "I understand, Marcus. And I'm willing to try. But you have to be honest with me. No more secrets."

"Agreed," he says, his voice firm. "No more secrets."

We drive in silence for a while, both of us lost in our thoughts. The city lights give way to darker streets as we approach my dad's neighborhood. My heart starts to race as we get closer, the reality of confronting my dad sinking in.

"We're almost there," Marcus says, his voice pulling me out of my thoughts.

I take a deep breath, steeling myself for what's to come. "I'm ready."

We pull up to my dad's house, the familiar sight of the rundown building sending a pang of sadness through me. This is where I grew up, where so much pain and struggle happened. But now, it's just another battleground in this war.

Marcus turns off the engine and looks at me. "Stay close to me. Let me handle him."

I nod, feeling a strange mix of fear and determination. "I will."

We step out of the car and walk up to the front door. Marcus knocks, the sound echoing in the quiet night. "Not in," he says. "You still got your key?"

"Under there," I say, motioning toward a plant pot filled with cigarette butts.

EIGHTEEN

Kelsey

We step inside, and the musty smell of neglect and old alcohol hits me like a physical force. The air is heavy with the scent of stale cigarette smoke and something rotten that I could never quite place.

I expect Marcus to look disgusted but his face shows no expression at all. I imagine, like last time he was here, he's comparing it to his penthouse, where everything is pristine and orderly.

Here, the walls are yellowed with age and grime, and the floors are covered in a layer of dirt and clutter.

There are boxes of electronics, clothes with the tags still on, and random knick-knacks that were probably worthless but stolen anyway.

Garbage bags are stacked against the walls, and old newspapers are scattered everywhere, their headlines faded and unreadable. The broken furniture and shattered glass make it clear that this place hasn't seen a decent day in years.

Marcus follows me through the mess, his eyes scanning the chaos with a cold, calculating gaze.

He looks completely out of place, like a polished gemstone in a pile of rubble. His presence is both reassuring and imposing, a stark reminder of the different world I now inhabit.

He stops at a dusty, broken picture frame lying facedown on a cluttered table. He picks it up, revealing a faded photograph of a woman with warm eyes and a gentle smile. The glass is cracked, but her kindness shines through.

"Is this your mother?" he asks, his voice softer now, almost gentle.

My throat tightens as I nod. "I thought he'd got rid of all her photos." I take a deep breath. "Yeah, that's her."

"Beautiful woman."

"Too good for my father. He charmed her, love-bombed her with gifts and attention. She thought she'd found her Prince Charming." I sigh, looking away from the picture. "But then he started controlling her financially, making sure she had to rely on him for everything."

Marcus sets the frame down carefully, his eyes never leaving mine. "What happened to her?"

"She got sick," I say, my voice barely above a whisper. The memories come flooding back, painful and vivid. "I've always suspected he had something to do with it, but I could never prove it.

"He was in charge of giving her the meds from the doctor. I always thought he maybe gave her too much or too little one day. She was supposed to be getting better but then she was gone."

I feel a tear slip down my cheek and quickly wipe it away, not wanting to show weakness. But Marcus's gaze softens, and he steps closer, his presence a strange comfort in this place of despair.

"She deserved better," he says. "And so did you."

He reaches out, his hand gently lifting my chin so I'm forced to meet his eyes. "You'll never have to live like this again," he adds firmly. "I promise you that."

His words are like a balm to my wounded soul. For the first time in a long time, I feel a glimmer of hope. I lean into his touch, the warmth of his hand a stark contrast to the cold, empty house around us.

The strength in his voice, the conviction in his eyes—it makes me want to believe him, to trust that I can finally leave this life behind.

Marcus's expression hardens, but there's a flicker of something softer beneath the surface. "You're mine now, Kelsey. That means protecting you, making sure you never have to deal with this kind of shit again."

I should be terrified by the possessiveness in his voice, the implication that I belong to him. But instead, I feel a strange comfort in his words, a sense of safety I haven't felt in years.

His eyes darken with anger. "He'll answer for everything," he says, his voice a dangerous promise.

Just then, the front door creaks open, and my father stumbles in, reeking of alcohol. He freezes when he sees us, his eyes wide with fear and confusion.

"Sit down," Marcus orders, his voice cold and commanding.

My father hesitates, and in an instant, Marcus strides over and smacks him hard across the face. The sound echoes through the room, and my father stumbles back, clutching his cheek.

"Sit. Down." Marcus's tone leaves no room for argument.

My father, dazed and frightened, collapses into a chair, blood trickling from the corner of his mouth. Marcus stands over him, a menacing figure of control and authority.

"What do you want?" my father slurs, his eyes darting nervously between us.

Marcus's gaze is unwavering. "We're here for answers," he says. "And you're going to give them to us."

NINETEEN

Kelsey
_____

Marcus's voice is low and menacing as he speaks to my father. "You have one chance to tell me where the necklace is."

I can see the shift in Marcus's eyes, such a transformation from the man who held me tenderly to the powerful, ruthless figure before me now.

My father looks up, defiance flashing in his eyes. "I don't know what you're talking about."

Without hesitation, Marcus grabs my father's hand and snaps one of his fingers. The sickening crack echoes through the room, and my father screams in pain, clutching his hand.

So often I wanted to see him hurt but now it's happening I just want it to be over.

"Nine more fingers," Marcus says calmly. "I'm good. I can break each one in two different places. A skill I've picked up over the years."

My father's face is twisted in agony as he looks up at Marcus. "How did you find out?"

Marcus smirks, a dark glint in his eyes. "Andrew broke. You will too. Now talk."

My father's shoulders slump in defeat. "I hid it."

Marcus's grip tightens on my father's hand. "Where exactly?"

My father stammers, struggling to provide specifics. "It's in the old wing of Bellevue Hospital. I hid it inside a refrigerator, behind some old medical equipment. Room 14."

Marcus turns to me, his eyes intense. "What should we do with him? If we let him go, he might come back to bite us. If we kill him, there are no loose ends."

I freeze, the weight of the decision crashing down on me. I look at my father, broken and terrified, and my heart aches with a mixture of anger and pity.

Despite everything he's done, he's still my father. "Let him live," I say finally, my voice trembling. "But he has to disappear. Far away, where he can't hurt anyone else."

Marcus nods, respecting my decision. He pulls out a gun, and my father's eyes widen in fear.

"Did you kill Kelsey's mother?" Marcus asks, his voice deadly calm. "She might want to let you live but I make the decisions in this marriage. I can make it easy or really fucking painful. Did you kill your wife?"

In a desperate move, my father lunges for the gun. Time seems to slow as Marcus effortlessly sidesteps him, knocking him to the ground. My father lies there, gasping for breath, defeated and broken.

Marcus looks at me, his eyes softening for a moment. "We need to know the truth, Kelsey. If he killed your mother, he deserves to pay for it."

Tears blur my vision as I nod, the reality of the situation sinking in. "Please, Dad," I plead. "Just tell me the truth for once in your life."

"You're dying either way," Marcus says. "Tell the truth and I'll make it quick."

My father looks up at me, his eyes filled with a mix of regret and defiance.

"I didn't kill her," he mutters. "But I didn't save her either. I was too drunk to make sure she got the right doses." He looks at me with genuine pain in his eyes. "I'm sorry, you both deserved better than me."

He lunges for the gun again. "No, don't," I cry out as he snatches it.

Before I can say anything else, Dad puts it to his own head and pulls the trigger.

TWENTY

Kelsey

The gunshot echoes in my ears. For a moment I feel nothing. I stare at my father's lifeless body as it crashes into bags of garbage, the pistol still clutched in his hand.

A wave of nausea and panic crashes over me, like I'm teetering on the edge of an abyss with no way back.

Marcus steps forward, his movements measured and deliberate. He kneels beside my father, checking for any sign of life. It's a futile gesture, and we both know it.

He stands, his expression a mask of control, though I can see the glint of something deeper in his eyes. Perhaps pleasure? Or simply the acceptance of yet another dark deed done.

"Kelsey," he says softly, his voice cutting through the fog of my thoughts. "We need to go. Someone will have heard the shot."

I nod, my legs trembling as I force them to move. He takes my arm, guiding me out of the house. The cold night air hits me like a slap, a stark contrast to the suffocating heat inside. I breathe it in, trying to steady myself, trying to make sense of the chaos swirling in my mind.

We reach the car, and Marcus opens the door for me. I slide into the passenger seat, my hands shaking as I clutch the seatbelt. Marcus gets in beside me.

He starts the engine, and we pull away from the house, leaving behind the last remnants of my old life. I look down. I'm still holding the photo of my mother.

Silence fills the car, heavy and oppressive. The sound of the gunshot replays in my head, a haunting reminder of what just happened. My father is dead. Killed himself.

Why can't I cry?

I glance at Marcus, his profile sharp and unreadable in the dim light. His hands grip the steering wheel with a controlled strength that both reassures and frightens me.

I wonder how he can be so composed after everything that's happened. How he can navigate this world of darkness and death with such ease.

"Why can't I cry?" I ask out loud. "I don't feel anything at all. What's wrong with me?"

"There are no absolutes in this world, Kelsey," he finally says. "Only shades of gray. Every decision, every action, it's all a matter of perspective. You hated him and you loved him. You wanted him dead and you wanted him alive. You want to cry but you feel nothing."

His words hang in the air, heavy with meaning. I think about my father, about the life he led, the choices he made. About

Marcus and the choices he's made. About me and the choices I'm being forced to make. Nothing is black and white. It's all a murky gray, a tangled web of morality and necessity.

"Is that supposed to help?" I ask, my voice trembling.

"No," Marcus admits. "It doesn't. But it's the reality we live in. You learn to accept it, or it destroys you."

I turn to look at him, searching his face for any sign of the man beneath the mask. I see flashes of something—pain, regret, maybe even vulnerability. It's fleeting, but it's there. Despite the power and control he wields, Marcus is just as trapped by this life as I am.

"I don't know if I can accept it," I confess, my voice breaking. "My dad just killed himself."

Marcus reaches over, taking my hand in his. His touch is surprisingly gentle, a stark contrast to the violence he's capable of. "Accept it or give up. You want to give up?"

I want to believe him. I want to believe that I can find strength in this chaos, that I can carve out a place for myself in this world. But the doubt lingers, a constant shadow.

"Why did you do it?" I ask, needing to understand.

"Do what?"

"You were going to kill him, weren't you? He only did it to stop you doing it."

Marcus's grip tightens on my hand, his eyes darkening. "He was a threat. He would have continued to hurt you, to use you. And because in this world, sometimes you have to make hard choices. That's my life."

"I told you to let him live."

"I know but I'm in charge around here, not you. I make the final decision."

My father was a monster, a man who thrived on control and violence. But does that justify his death? Does it make Marcus's actions right? Or is it just another shade of gray in this twisted reality?

"I should hate you," I whisper, my voice filled with a mix of anger and confusion. "I should want to kill you for what you did."

"But you don't, do you?" Marcus says softly, his eyes locking onto mine. "Because deep down, you know that this is the only way to survive in this world."

I look away, unable to hold his gaze. He's right. As much as I want to deny it, I understand. I understand the need for control, the need for power. It scares me how easily I'm starting to see the world through his eyes. Because he's right. I am grateful for his control. My father can't hurt me anymore.

TWENTY-ONE

Kelsey

"You got any water?" I ask about twenty minutes later.

"Check the glovebox," Marcus replies.

I open the glovebox and find a bottle of water next to a small bag of cat treats. "Seriously?" I say, holding them up. "You carry cat treats?"

Marcus shrugs. "Barney has his needs, same as the rest of us."

"Never would have you figured for such a cat lover."

"We're almost at the hospital," he replies, his tone shifting to a more serious one. "We'll find out soon enough if your dad was telling the truth."

I feel a knot form in my stomach. "Marcus, what if it's a trap? What if my dad lied?"

Marcus glances at me, his expression unreadable. "Are you worried about me? You sound worried."

"Of course I am," I say, my voice a mix of frustration and concern. "I don't want you to walk into something dangerous. There's been enough deaths tonight."

He smirks. "I thought you were hoping I'd die so you could inherit my wealth."

I cringe, thinking of Rafael's offer. I force a smile on my lips. "Please, you're way too paranoid. Besides, you'll probably die of old age before I ever see a penny. About five years time, yeah, old man?"

Marcus laughs, a genuine, hearty laugh that surprises me. "If my hearing wasn't so bad in my old age, I might have been offended there. Now, I need you to follow my orders when we park up."

"I can't just sit back and do nothing," I protest. "I want to be involved."

He shakes his head. "Not if it puts you in danger. Stay in the car, Kelsey. That's not up for negotiation."

I glare at him, my frustration boiling over. "You can't keep me out of everything. If I'm part of this, I need to know what's going on. You might need back up."

Marcus's expression softens slightly. "I understand that, but your safety comes first. You have to trust me on this."

I sigh, feeling the weight of the situation pressing down on me. "Fine. But don't think I'm happy about it."

"Duly noted," he says, pulling the car to a stop. "We're here."

We step out of the car, and I take in our surroundings. The location is desolate, an abandoned section of the hospital on the outskirts of the city. Marcus walks around the car, coming to stand close to me.

"Remember, stay in the car," he says firmly.

"I remember," I mutter, crossing my arms.

He gives me one last look before heading towards the derelict wing. I watch him go, my heart pounding in my chest. The mix of fear, frustration, and something else—something deeper—swirls inside me.

I watch him disappear into the darkness, and I find myself praying that he comes back safe.

The thought of losing him, as infuriating as he can be, is something I can't bear. Not now, when he's all I have left to cling to.

TWENTY-TWO

Kelsey

I sit in the car, my fingers drumming nervously on the steering wheel. Each minute drags by, feeling like an eternity. I keep glancing at the door Marcus disappeared through, hoping to see him emerge safe and sound, but there's nothing.

I can't stand it any longer. Every instinct in me screams to stay put, to follow Marcus's orders, but I can't. The worry gnawing at my insides becomes unbearable.

Without another thought, I open the car door and step out into the open air, my heart pounding in my ears.

I stride toward the old wing, the imposing structure looming ahead. The closer I get, the more I sense that something is off, a chill running down my spine.

As I push open the creaking door, the musty smell of neglect and decay hits me. I pause for a moment, taking in the eerie silence. Dust motes float in the dim light filtering through broken windows, and the faint sound of dripping water echoes through the empty halls.

I move cautiously, my footsteps echoing in the empty corridors. The hospital is a maze of abandoned rooms and decaying equipment. I notice boot marks on the dusty floor, leading deeper into the building. My pulse quickens as I follow them, hoping they will lead me to Marcus.

As I round a corner, I see a door slightly ajar. The number 14 is barely visible on the rusted plaque. I push the door open and peer inside, my breath catching in my throat.

The room is filled with old medical equipment, and in the corner stands a refrigerator, its power cord trailing to a hidden outlet.

My heart races as I realize Marcus is in the room, his tall frame silhouetted against the dim light. He's focused, intent on his task, and completely unaware of my presence. He bends down, reaching for the refrigerator handle.

"Marcus, stop!" I call out, my voice echoing in the empty room.

He turns, his expression instantly darkening with anger. "What the hell are you doing here?" he snaps, his voice low and furious. "I told you to stay in the car. You're putting yourself in danger."

"Don't open that."

He steps closer, his eyes blazing with a mixture of anger and concern. "You don't understand the risks. This isn't a game, Kelsey. Go back to the car. Now. I checked a few rooms but there could be people hiding anywhere. You're not safe in here.."

"Neither are you." I stand my ground, my gaze fixed on the refrigerator. "Marcus, there's no power to this building."

"And?"

"So how is that fridge still running? Look at the temperature gauge on top – it's working. That doesn't make sense."

His expression shifts from anger to realization. He glances at the fridge, then back at me. "You're right. It doesn't add up."

I point to the floor, my finger tracing the thin, almost invisible wire running along the ground. "It's a trap. Someone set this up."

Marcus's jaw tightens as he looks at the wire, then back at me. "You might have just saved us both." He grabs my arm, pulling me away from the fridge. "But you need to listen to me. This is dangerous. Go back to the car and wait for me there."

"I'm not leaving you," I insist, my voice steady. "We're in this together."

He lets out a frustrated sigh but doesn't argue further. Instead, he turns his attention to the wire, carefully tracing its path to a hidden mechanism behind the fridge.

"You'd be dead if I stayed in the car," I snap. "A thank you would be nice."

His eyes are sharp as he scans the wire, his expression turning grim. "I can disarm this," he says, his voice calm but filled with a steely determination. He looks up at me, his eyes softening for a moment. "But you need to stay back. I don't want you getting hurt."

I nod, my heart pounding in my chest. "Just... be careful, okay?" I whisper, my voice shaky with worry. "We can't afford to lose each other."

He stands, his gaze meeting mine. For a moment, the world narrows to just the two of us. The tension, the danger, it all fades away as he steps closer. His hand cups my cheek, his thumb brushing gently against my skin.

"I promise," he murmurs, leaning in. His lips meet mine in a tender, yet urgent kiss, and I feel a warmth spread through me, filling me with love and a deep concern for him.

As he pulls away, the world snaps back into focus. The wire, the danger— all still there. He kneels down, his focus shifting entirely to the trap in front of him.

His fingers move with careful precision, tracing the wire to its source. I watch, my breath held, as he works. His movements are methodical, almost mechanical, as if he's done this a hundred times before.

He pulls out a small tool from his pocket, a multi-tool with a set of fine-tipped pliers. With a steady hand, he carefully strips the wire, revealing several smaller colored ones inside. He snips one, then another.

Each cut is deliberate, calculated. I can see the tension in his shoulders, the tightness in his jaw. He's fully focused, every muscle in his body coiled and ready. The air feels heavy, the silence thick with anticipation.

"Red or green?" he asks, holding the ends of the final two. "What do you think?"

"You don't know?"

"Course I do," he replies. "Just thought I'd make it fun."

With a final, decisive snip of the red wire, he visibly relaxes. He looks up at me, a small, reassuring smile tugging at the corner of his mouth. "Now, let's see what we've got here."

He moves to the refrigerator, his expression serious once more. He pulls it open, revealing a pile of empty bottles and jars inside. He pushes them aside and finds what he's looking for. A wooden box at the back. He reaches in, pulling out the box and opening it. Inside is a note. His eyes narrow as he unfolds it, his jaw clenching tightly.

For a moment, he doesn't say anything, his eyes scanning the words on the page. The tension in the air thickens, and I feel a knot form in my stomach. Whatever's written there, it's not good. Marcus's face darkens, the warmth from our earlier kiss gone, replaced by a cold, hard edge.

He hands me the note, his fingers brushing mine as he does. "Read it," he says, his voice low and dangerous. I take the paper, unfolding it carefully. My eyes skim over the scrawled handwriting, each word a punch to the gut.

Nice try, Marcus, it reads. *You thought it would be that easy? You're playing my game now, and you're losing. I'm having so much fun, got to tell you. Call me if you want to talk. Be prepared to grovel. - Hawke*

A chill runs down my spine as I read the note, my hands shaking slightly. I look up at Marcus, who is staring at the ground, his jaw clenched so tight I worry he'll crack a tooth. The controlled calm from before is gone, replaced by a simmering rage just beneath the surface.

"We're going to make him pay for this," he says, his voice a dangerous whisper. There's a fire in his eyes, a determination that sends a shiver through me. The man he was is gone. All that's left is the devil that hides inside.

TWENTY-THREE

Kelsey

Marcus's face is a mask of frustration as we drive away from the old wing of Bellevue Hospital. He slams his hand against the steering wheel, his knuckles white with rage.

"Fuck!" he growls, his eyes blazing with intensity. "That was so damn close. I was sure it was there."

I reach out, placing my hand on his arm, trying to calm him down. "Marcus, it's okay. We got out of there. We're alive, right?"

He shoots me a glare, his jaw clenched tight. "You should've stayed in the car, Kelsey. You disobeyed me and put yourself in danger."

I take a deep breath, trying to keep my own frustration in check as he lashes out. "Marcus, I couldn't just sit there. I knew something was wrong. If I hadn't gone in, you might be dead right now."

He shakes his head, anger and something else—fear,

maybe—clouding his eyes. "You don't get it. I make the choices. I'm the one who decides what happens."

"Really?" I snap, my own anger bubbling to the surface. "Because from where I was standing, your choice was about to get you killed. You're not used to working with others, I get that, but you need to start trusting me."

He pulls the car over to the side of the road, turning to face me fully. His eyes are intense, a storm brewing within them. "Trust you?" he says, his voice low and dangerous. "I've spent my whole life relying only on myself. Trusting others gets you killed."

I reach out, cupping his face in my hands. "Marcus, we're in this together now. You don't have to do everything alone. Let me help you."

For a moment, he just stares at me, the anger slowly ebbing away, replaced by something deeper, more vulnerable. He sighs, leaning his forehead against mine. "I'm not used to this," he admits. "I don't know how to let you in."

"You don't have to let go completely," I say softly. "Just enough to let me help you."

He closes his eyes, taking a deep breath. "I want you, Kelsey. I need you right now."

I smile, leaning in to kiss him gently. "Then take me," I whisper against his lips.

He responds instantly, his lips crashing against mine in a desperate, possessive kiss. The intensity of his need ignites a fire within me, one that I can't ignore. His hands roam over my body, pulling me closer as the kiss deepens.

I feel his desperation, his desire to claim and possess me, and it only fuels my own hunger. I kiss him back with equal fervor, my hands tangling in his hair as I press myself against him.

"Marcus," I gasp between kisses, my voice filled with longing. "I want you so much."

He growls softly, his hands gripping my hips as he pulls me into his lap. "You have no idea how much I need you right now," he murmurs against my lips.

We barely make it into the back seat of the car, our movements frantic and urgent. I straddle him, feeling his hardness pressing against me through our clothes. His hands slide up my thighs, pushing my skirt higher as he kisses me deeply.

"Tell me what you want, Kelsey," he says, his voice rough with desire.

I look into his eyes, feeling the raw intensity of his need. "I want your cock in my mouth," I say, my voice filled with hunger and desire.

He groans, his hands guiding me as I slide off his lap and kneel between his legs. I can see the anticipation in his eyes, the way his breath quickens as I reach for his belt. I unbuckle it slowly, teasing him as I pull down his zipper.

I free him from his pants, my eyes locked on his as I lean in and take him into my mouth. His hands tangle in my hair, guiding me as I work him with my lips and tongue. The taste of him, the feel of his hardness against my tongue, drives me wild.

"Fuck, Kelsey," he groans, his head falling back against the seat. "You're so fucking good at this."

I smile around him, the praise only spurring me on. I take him deeper, my hand stroking the base of his shaft as I hollow my cheeks and suck him hard. His moans fill the car, sounds of pleasure that make my own arousal pool between my legs.

With a final, deep thrust, he groans, his release powerful and overwhelming. I feel him spill into my mouth, the culmination of everything we've both been holding back. He shudders, his body taut with the intensity of his orgasm. I swallow, savoring the taste of him, the sense of satisfaction that comes with knowing I've pushed him over the edge.

As he comes down from the high, I pull back, wiping my lips and looking up at him. His eyes are dark and intense, still hazy with the remnants of his pleasure. There's a softness there too, a tenderness that surprises me. He reaches out, cupping my face and pulling me up for a kiss. It's gentle, almost reverent, a stark contrast to the heated passion of moments before.

But then his expression changes, a smoldering intensity taking over. "Now," he murmurs, his voice a low growl. "Touch yourself for me, Kelsey. I want to watch you come."

My heart races at his command, a thrill of excitement running through me. I settle back, my fingers finding their way between my legs. I part my thighs, feeling the slick heat of my arousal. His eyes never leave me, dark and hungry, as I begin to touch myself.

I circle my clit with slow, deliberate movements, the pleasure building with each stroke. His gaze is like a physical touch, amplifying every sensation. "That's it," he murmurs, his voice filled with approval. "Show me how good it feels."

I close my eyes, losing myself in the sensation. My breaths come in short, ragged gasps, my fingers moving faster as I chase my release. "Marcus," I moan, the sound a mix of need and pleasure.

"Come for me, Kelsey," he commands, his voice a dark promise. "I want to see you do it. The first night at mine, I watched from the doorway but I could see nothing. I wanted to fuck you so badly. Show me how you make yourself come."

His words push me over the edge. My orgasm crashes over me, my body trembling with the intensity of it. I cry out, my fingers still working as wave after wave of pleasure rolls through me. His eyes are locked on mine, a look of raw desire and satisfaction on his face.

As the aftershocks of my climax fade, I collapse back against the seat, breathless and spent. He reaches for me, pulling me into his arms. The car is filled with the sound of our heavy breathing, the aftermath of our shared passion.

For a moment, we simply hold each other, the world outside forgotten. Then he brushes a strand of hair from my face, his touch tender. "You're incredible," he murmurs, his lips brushing against my forehead.

I smile, feeling a warmth spread through me. "So are you," I reply, my voice soft. "It's good to be alive, isn't it?"

He nods, his eyes filled with a mix of emotions. "Yes, it is."

We drive home in a comfortable silence, the tension between us slowly dissipating with each passing mile. The anticipation crackles between us, an electric charge that only grows as we approach the penthouse.

As soon as we step inside, the elevator barely closes behind us before we're on each other. The need is immediate and overwhelming, an unspoken agreement that neither of us can deny.

Marcus's hands are on me, his touch urgent and possessive. He pulls me close, his mouth finding mine in a searing kiss that leaves me breathless. I respond eagerly, my hands tugging at his shirt, desperate to feel his skin against mine.

The fabric tears slightly as I yank it over his head, revealing the hard planes of his chest. My fingers trace the lines of his muscles, marveling at the strength beneath.

His hands aren't idle either. He grips the hem of my top, pulling it up and over my head in one swift motion. He discards it carelessly, his eyes darkening with desire as they roam over my exposed skin.

"You're so beautiful," he murmurs, his voice low and husky. The compliment sends a thrill through me, making my heart race faster.

I reach for his belt, fumbling with the buckle in my haste. He chuckles softly, a sound that's both teasing and filled with heat. "Impatient, are we?" he taunts, but he helps me with the buckle, pushing his pants down his hips.

I follow suit, stripping off my own clothes and kicking them aside. We're a flurry of movement, our things piling up haphazardly on the floor, a testament to our desperate need.

His hands are on me again, sliding over the curves of my hips, tugging down my underwear. I shiver at the cool air against my bare skin, but the heat of his gaze makes me forget everything else.

He lifts me effortlessly, cradling me against his chest as he carries me to the bedroom. I wrap my arms around his neck, burying my face in the crook of his shoulder, inhaling his scent—a mix of cologne and something uniquely him.

We collapse onto the bed, a tangle of limbs and heated breaths. He hovers over me, his eyes locked onto mine with an intensity that makes my pulse quicken. His hands roam over my body, touching and caressing every inch of skin. He takes his time, exploring me with a reverence that makes me feel worshiped.

He leans down, his mouth trailing hot kisses along my collarbone, down the valley between my breasts. His hands cup them, kneading gently as his lips close around one nipple. I gasp, arching into his touch, my fingers tangling in his hair. He sucks and nips, sending jolts of pleasure straight to my core.

"Marcus," I moan, my voice breathless and needy. He moves lower, his tongue tracing a path down my stomach, stopping just above the place where I need him most. My hips lift instinctively, seeking his touch, but he holds me down, a wicked smile playing on his lips.

"Patience," he murmurs, his voice like velvet, sending shivers down my spine. The word hangs in the air, thick with promise and desire. He kisses the inside of my thigh, the touch feather-light, his breath warm against my skin. I gasp, my fingers digging into the sheets as I arch toward him, seeking more of his tantalizing touch.

He moves to my other thigh, his lips grazing the sensitive skin, leaving a trail of heat in their wake. Every kiss is a promise, a tease, a maddening delay of the pleasure I crave. The anticipation is electric, every nerve ending alive and tingling, every cell in my body screaming for release.

He looks up at me, his eyes dark with desire, a smirk playing at the corners of his mouth. "You're so beautiful like this," he says, his voice a low, seductive purr. "So eager, so needy."

I whimper, my body trembling with want. "Please," I beg, my voice barely more than a breathless whisper. "I need you."

"Not yet," he replies, his tone teasing, almost playful. "I want to savor this."

He continues his slow, deliberate journey up my thighs, his kisses growing bolder, more insistent. Each touch sends a jolt of pleasure through me, my anticipation building to a fever pitch. I can feel the heat pooling between my legs, my arousal slick and undeniable.

Finally, finally, he gives in to my silent pleas. His mouth finds my most sensitive spot, his tongue flicking out to taste me. I cry out, my fingers tightening in his hair as he devours me with an almost primal hunger. The sensation is overwhelming, a rush of pleasure that leaves me gasping, my body arching off the bed.

He alternates between long, slow licks and quick, teasing flicks, driving me wild with need. His tongue moves with expert precision, finding every spot that makes me moan, every touch sending a new wave of pleasure crashing through me. My hands clench in his hair, urging him on, my breaths coming in ragged gasps.

Just when I think I can't take any more, his fingers join in, sliding inside me with a delicious ease. They curl, finding that perfect spot, and I see stars. My body tenses, my muscles tightening around him as he works me closer and closer to the edge.

"You taste so sweet," he murmurs against me, his voice a low growl that vibrates through my core. "So perfect."

I can't form words, can't do anything but feel. The pleasure is all-consuming, a white-hot fire that burns through me, leaving me trembling and desperate. I'm close, so close, every nerve stretched to its limit.

"Marcus," I gasp, my voice shaking. "I'm going to—"

"Yes," he growls, his fingers thrusting deeper, his tongue moving faster. "Come for me, Kelsey. Let go."

The orgasm crashes over me, a tidal wave of pleasure that leaves me shaking, my cries echoing through the room. He doesn't stop, doesn't relent, driving me higher and higher until I'm lost in the sensation, my mind blank with ecstasy.

As the waves of pleasure finally begin to subside, he slows his movements, his touch gentle and soothing. He kisses his way back up my body, his lips soft and warm against my flushed skin. When he reaches my lips, he kisses me deeply, and I can taste myself on him, a reminder of the pleasure he just gave me.

"You're incredible," he murmurs against my lips, his voice filled with awe and adoration. "Absolutely incredible. And I'm not done with you yet."

His words send a fresh wave of desire through me, my body already craving more. As he moves to position himself above me, I know that this is only the beginning.

As the aftershocks fade, I can taste myself on his lips, a heady reminder of what just happened. He settles between my legs, his hard length pressing against my pussy. I wrap my legs around him, pulling him closer, needing him inside me.

He pauses, looking down at me with a tender expression that makes my heart ache. "Are you ready?" he asks, his voice soft.

"Yes," I whisper, my hands gripping his shoulders. "I want you in me. I want a baby with you."

He enters me slowly, filling me completely. The sensation is exquisite, a mix of pleasure and a sweet, almost painful fullness. We stay like that for a moment, savoring the connection, the feeling of being completely joined. Then he starts to move, setting a slow, steady rhythm that drives me wild.

"God, you feel so good," he groans, his hands gripping my hips.

I cling to him, lost in the sensation, the sheer bliss of having him inside me. We move together, our bodies in perfect sync, each thrust sending sparks of pleasure through me. His mouth finds mine in a searing kiss, our tongues tangling, our breaths mingling.

As the tension builds, he pulls back slightly, looking down at me with a fierce intensity. "I want to see you pregnant," he murmurs, his voice rough with desire. "I want to see you round with our child, your tits full and heavy."

The image sends a jolt of heat through me. The thought of carrying his child, of creating a life together, is both thrilling and terrifying. "Yes," I gasp, my nails digging into his back. "I want that too. I want to give you everything."

He increases his pace, his thrusts becoming more urgent, more demanding. "I'll fill you up," he growls, his voice thick with promise. "I'll make sure you get pregnant. We'll have a beautiful family."

The words push me closer to the edge, the idea of being with him, of creating a future together, adding to the pleasure. I can feel myself tightening around him, my body coiling like a spring. He feels it too, his movements becoming more frantic, more desperate.

"Come for me," he commands, his voice a mix of desire and authority. "Come for me again, Kelsey."

His words, the feel of him inside me, the intensity of the moment—it's all too much. I shatter beneath him, my orgasm ripping through me with a force that leaves me breathless. I cry out his name, my body trembling with the force of my release.

He follows me over the edge, his body tensing, his hands gripping my hips tightly. He groans, a deep, guttural sound, as he finds his release. I can feel the warmth of his cum filling me, the culmination of everything we've been building towards.

We collapse against each other, our bodies spent, our breaths coming in ragged gasps. He pulls me close, his arms wrapping around me, holding me tightly. I bury my face in his neck, inhaling his scent, feeling the steady beat of his heart against mine.

For a moment, we just lie there, tangled together, our bodies still humming with the aftershocks of our release.

Then he pulls me close, his arms wrapping around me protectively. "You're my wife," he whispers, his voice filled with emotion. "Not just my purchase. I'm sorry for how I've treated you tonight. I shouldn't have yelled at you."

I look up at him, my heart swelling with emotion. "You've been hurt before, same as me. I get it. But we have to work together, okay?"

He nods, his eyes filled with determination. "I promise, Kelsey. We'll do this together. I'll keep my word."

TWENTY-FOUR

Marcus

I sit alone in the dimly lit living room, the city sprawled out beneath me, its lights twinkling like stars. The silence of the night wraps around me, broken only by the soft purring of Barney.

He's perched on my lap, content as I absentmindedly stroke his fur. My thoughts are a tangled mess, circling around the one thing I can't seem to shake—fatherhood.

The idea of being a dad both excites and terrifies me. What kind of father will I be? The question haunts me, and I fear the answer. I killed her father. I've killed so many people.

Should a man like me ever become a father? But if I don't do this, will my empire crumble when I die? Will Hawke take it all over?

I gaze out at the cityscape, the weight of my past pressing down on me. My father was a violent man, his hands quick to punish. What if I turn out the same? The thought of raising a hand to my child fills me with a cold dread. But could I stop myself?

As I sit lost in thought, I hear soft footsteps behind me. I don't turn around, but I know it's Kelsey. She always moves so quietly, like a whisper. She stops beside me, placing a gentle hand on my shoulder.

"What's wrong, Marcus?" she asks, her voice soft and concerned. "Can't sleep?"

I shake my head, forcing a small smile. "I'm fine. You should go back to bed."

She doesn't move. "I can tell something's up," she insists, her tone gentle but firm. "Talk to me. Please."

I hesitate, torn between keeping my fears to myself and opening up to her. Finally, I take a deep breath and meet her eyes.

"Are you afraid of me, Kelsey?" The question slips out before I can stop it, and I hold my breath, waiting for her response.

Her brows furrow in confusion. "Afraid of you? No, not anymore," she says with a shake of her head. "I trust you, Marcus. Why would you think otherwise?"

I sigh, looking away. "I'm scared," I admit, the words feeling heavy on my tongue. "Scared of what I might do, of hurting our child. My father was a very violent man. What if I become like him? What if I can't control myself around our child?"

"You ever thought about hitting me?"

"No, of course not."

Kelsey kneels beside me, her hand slipping into mine. Her touch is warm, grounding me. "Marcus," she says softly, "you've never given me any reason to fear you. Not once. The thought of you hitting me or our child, it never even enters my head. All you've done is protect me." She turns her forearm toward me. "Look at the bruises, fading away, never to return. Thanks to you."

I search her eyes, looking for any sign of doubt, but all I see is sincerity. It eases some of the tension in my chest, but not all of it. "I'm not sure I'll make a good dad," I confess. "I don't know if I have it in me."

She squeezes my hand, her gaze unwavering. "You've already shown me what kind of person you are," she says, her voice filled with warmth. "You took me from a horrible life, gave me a chance to start over. You've been nothing but kind to me.

"You've offered to put me through university, bought your mom's bookstore so the staff kept their jobs... Marcus, you've done so many good things. You're a better person than you think. Look at Barney, you think he'd hang around if you were an asshole?"

I feel a lump form in my throat, the sincerity in her words cutting through my self-doubt. "I feed him, that's all cats need."

"Why do you think you're such a bad person?" she asks, her eyes searching mine.

I swallow hard, the memories of my past clawing at the edges of my mind. "Because of the things I've done," I admit. "I've hurt people, made choices I'm not proud of. Sometimes, I think there's no coming back from that."

She shakes her head, a small, sad smile on her lips. "Everyone has a past, Marcus. We all make mistakes. But that doesn't define who you are now or who you can become. You have the power to be different, to be better. You choose whether it affects who you are now."

"You don't know the truth about me." I take a deep breath, gathering my thoughts. "I had a half sister. She was murdered by Hawke's men. They poisoned her. She died in my arms. My father blamed me. Told me I didn't care about her because we had different mothers. Told me I should have saved her."

"How old were you?"

"Twelve."

She reaches out and places a hand on mine, her touch grounding me. "I'm so sorry, Marcus. That must have been horrible."

"It was," I admit, my voice raw with emotion. "I hunted down the men who poisoned her. She'd gone to some bar, underage, and they'd spiked her drink but put too much shit in it. I tortured them then I killed them. I made sure it hurt when they died. Afterward I found out they worked for Hawke. He's been after revenge ever since. Says he always protects his family."

Kelsey's grip tightens, and I can see the pain in her eyes. "No wonder you're so determined to protect yours."

I nod, feeling a surge of emotion. "I've done a lot of terrible things since then, Kelsey. Formed a river of blood. I understand if you don't want children with me."

We sit in silence for a moment, the weight of my confession hanging in the air. Barney curls up on the floor, leaving us alone in our shared pain.

"I thought I was destined to live with my father forever," she replies. "Never imagined I could be free until you came along. You gave me hope. I've heard from people, the way they talk about you. You've done good things for many people. You're more than you think you are."

She sighs, smiling warmly. "We need to be different kinds of parents," she adds. "Better than ours were. We'll give our children the love and security we never had."

I reach out and cup her face in my hands, my heart swelling with a mixture of love and determination. "Are you sure?"

She leans into my touch, her eyes searching mine. "I'm sure."

I pull her into a deep kiss, my lips claiming hers with a fervor that leaves us both breathless. The kiss is more than just a declaration of ownership; it's a promise of everything I want to build with her.

She melts into me, her body responding to my touch, and I feel a surge of desire and love.

"I love you, Kelsey," I say.

"I love you too, Marcus," she replies and I believe her.

TWENTY-FIVE

Marcus

The morning air is crisp on the penthouse balcony, and the scent of freshly brewed coffee mingles with the tantalizing aroma of our breakfast spread. Barney lies lazily on the cushioned chair beside us, purring contentedly as he basks in the sunlight.

Kelsey sits across from me, her eyes sparkling with the morning light. She looks radiant, her hair catching the sunlight and her smile brightening my world. She catches me staring and raises an eyebrow.

"What?" she asks with a teasing smile, her voice light and playful.

"Nothing," I say, shaking my head with a grin. "Just admiring how beautiful you are."

She blushes, ducking her head slightly. "You're cheesy," she replies, reaching for her coffee. The simple act of watching her, the way she delicately holds the cup and takes a sip, fills me with a sense of peace.

"I'm going to call Hawke," I tell her. "It's time we arrange a meeting to get the necklace back."

She sets her cup down, her expression turning serious. "Are you sure about this?" she asks, her voice tinged with concern. "Do you really think we can trust him?"

I nod, though the tension in my gut suggests otherwise. "I don't trust Hawke as far as I can throw him," I admit. "But we don't have much choice. I need that necklace, and this is the only way I'm going to get it back."

She bites her lip, her eyes searching mine. "Just... be careful, okay?" she says softly. "I don't want anything to happen to you."

I reach across the table, taking her hand in mine. "I'll be careful," I promise, squeezing her hand reassuringly.

She nods, though the worry in her eyes doesn't fade. I release her hand and pull out my phone, dialing Hawke's number. The line rings a few times before a voice answers.

"Yes?" The voice is smooth, almost bored, but there's an underlying tension that I don't miss. It's Hawke's consigliere.

"It's Marcus," I say, my tone firm and authoritative. "I'm calling to arrange a meeting with your boss."

There's a brief pause, and I can almost hear the gears turning in the consigliere's head. "Marcus," he finally says, his tone shifting to something more formal. "Mr. Hawke has been expecting your call. He agrees to meet in person."

I exchange a glance with Kelsey, who nods slightly, her expression unreadable. "Good," I reply, keeping my voice steady. "Where and when?"

The consigliere hesitates for a moment, then responds, "Tomorrow evening, 8 PM, our place. Come alone."

I suppress a bitter laugh. "You and I both know I'm not walking into a trap without backup," I say, a hint of amusement in my voice. "I'll bring my men, and Hawke can bring his. We'll keep it civil."

There's another pause, and then the consigliere sighs. "Fine," he concedes. "But if anything goes wrong, Marcus, remember: you were the one who broke the agreement. You'll be the one to pay the price. You'll never see the necklace again."

I end the call and set the phone down, feeling the weight of the impending meeting settle heavily on my shoulders. Kelsey watches me, her expression concerned but resolute.

"So, it's happening," she says, more a statement than a question.

"Yeah," I nod, running a hand through my hair. "It's happening."

She stands up and moves around the table, slipping into my lap and wrapping her arms around my neck. I hold her close, inhaling the comforting scent of her. "We'll get through this," she whispers, her lips brushing against my ear. "Just like we always do."

I pull back slightly to look into her eyes. "You're not coming to the meeting," I state firmly. "It's too dangerous."

She narrows her eyes, a stubborn glint flashing in them. "Marcus, I'm not just going to sit at home while you go off to face Hawke," she argues, her voice firm. "I'm a part of this too, whether you like it or not. We agreed."

I sigh, cupping her cheek with my hand. "Kelsey, I need you safe," I say, my voice softening. "I can't focus if I'm worried about you."

She leans into my touch, her eyes softening. "And I can't just sit by and do nothing," she counters. "I know it's dangerous, but I'm willing to take that risk. We started this together, and we should see it through together."

I stare into her eyes, seeing the determination there. It mirrors my own. With a reluctant sigh, I nod. "All right," I concede. "But you're staying close to me the entire time. No wandering off."

She smiles, a triumphant glint in her eyes. "Deal," she agrees.

We sit there for a moment, the city sprawling out before us, the sun climbing higher in the sky. I tighten my hold on Kelsey, pressing a kiss to her forehead. No matter what happens tomorrow, we'll face it together. And with her by my side, I feel like we can handle anything.

She nods, a determined glint in her eyes. "We need to strategize our next moves. A direct confrontation might be too risky."

I consider her words. Kelsey has learned a lot fast about mafia affairs, her instincts sharpening with every passing hour. "What do you suggest?"

"Poisoning him," she says without hesitation. "We can control the situation better that way. Seems appropriate too, after what happened to your sister."

"What kind of poison?"

"How about this?" She pulls a vial from her pocket.

"Where did you get that?"

"Hawke gave it to me. Wanted me to put it in your drink. Offered to pay me handsomely if I did."

I take the vial from her, examining the contents. "You could have killed me anytime. You're my wife, you'd inherit all my money. Why didn't you get rid of me?"

"You need me to answer that?"

I nod. "I do."

"First, I wasn't sure about you. Then I was sure."

"Sure about what?"

"That you deserve a chance. You're a fucked up man, Marcus. Same as I'm a fucked up woman in a fucked up world. Why kill you for that?"

Her honesty hits me hard. "Alright. "We'll need to transfer the poison to a different container. Hawke needs to believe he's watching you pour it into my drink while it's actually going into his. How good a liar are you?"

"Told you I'd respect you after we slept together, didn't I?" She winks.

"If we fuck this up, we're both dead. I'm being serious."

"Then we better not fuck it up, right?"

TWENTY-SIX

Kelsey

The sprawling Hawke estate looms ahead, its grand façade shrouded in shadows cast by the setting sun.

As the car rolls to a stop, I take a deep breath, steeling myself for the confrontation ahead. Marcus squeezes my hand briefly before we step out of the car, a silent reminder that we're in this together.

Behind us, come half a dozen men, all unsmiling, all ready for a confrontation.

Hawke himself greets us all at the door, his smile slick and insincere. He's a tall, lean man with a predatory glint in his eyes, dressed in an impeccably tailored suit that only serves to amplify the aura of danger around him.

"Marcus," he purrs, extending a hand. "It's been too long."

Marcus accepts the handshake, his expression carefully neutral. "Not long enough," he replies coolly, his eyes never leaving Hawke's. The tension between them crackles like static electricity, the weight of their shared history palpable in the air.

Hawke chuckles, a low, oily sound. "Ever the charmer," he remarks, turning his gaze to me. "And here's the lovely Kelsey. So wonderful to see you again."

I force a polite smile, feeling a chill run down my spine as his eyes rake over me. "A pleasure," I manage, my voice steady despite the unease churning in my gut.

"Please, come in," Hawke says, gesturing for us to follow him into the mansion.

We walk through opulent halls adorned with expensive art and priceless antiques, a stark contrast to the darkness that seems to seep from every corner.

Finally, we enter a lavish conference room, dominated by a long, mahogany table and a wall of floor-to-ceiling windows overlooking the manicured gardens. In the furthest corner stand several of Hawke's men, all shooting daggers at us with their eyes.

Hawke walks to the head of the table, reaching into his pocket with a practiced flourish. He pulls out the necklace, the diamonds glittering under the chandelier's light.

"A gesture of good faith," he says smoothly, holding it up for us to see. "Now, let's talk business."

Marcus's eyes narrow slightly, but his face remains unreadable. He sits down, motioning for me to do the same. I settle into the chair beside him, trying to maintain an air of calm.

"Let's make this quick," Marcus says, his voice clipped. "I don't want to be here long."

Hawke raises an eyebrow, a sly smile playing at the corners of his lips. "Always straight to the point, aren't you? Very well."

He sets the necklace on the table and leans back in his chair, steepling his fingers. "I'm proposing a partnership, Marcus. It's time we put our differences aside and focus on what really matters—making money.

"Together, we could control this city, end the pointless bloodshed, and increase our profits tenfold."

Marcus's gaze flicks to me briefly, a silent exchange passing between us. His eyes are hard, a glimmer of something dangerous lurking beneath the surface.

He turns back to Hawke, a small, humorless smile on his lips. "You want me to work with you after your men murdered my sister?" he says, his voice dangerously soft. The air grows colder, the atmosphere heavy with the weight of unspoken threats.

Hawke's smile fades, replaced by a calculating look. "Ah, yes, the tragic fate of Maria," he says, feigning regret. "But let's not forget, Marcus, you buried six of my men alive for that, with their limbs broken so they couldn't climb out as the dirt was piled on. Family men. Good men. I'd say that makes us even."

A tense silence follows his words, the room thick with the ghosts of past violence. I glance at Marcus, his jaw clenched, his fists resting on the table, knuckles white.

For a moment, I fear he'll lose control, that the fragile truce will shatter before our eyes. But then, he takes a deep breath, visibly forcing himself to relax.

"Even," he echoes, his voice a low growl. "We'll call it even. But this partnership—" He pauses, his eyes cold and sharp as they lock onto Hawke's. "This partnership is on my terms."

Hawke's lips twitch into a smirk. "Of course," he says smoothly. "Whatever you need to make you feel comfortable."

My eyes wander to the drinks cabinet in the corner by Hawke's men, filled with an array of spirits that gleam under the room's soft lighting.

Hawke catches my gaze and smirks, a knowing glint in his eye. "Shall we toast to our new arrangement?" he suggests, his voice smooth and confident. He glances at me with a mischievous wink. "Perhaps your wife could do the honors?"

Marcus gives me a subtle nod, a silent agreement. I rise from my seat, forcing a composed smile as I make my way to the cabinet.

The bottles reflect the light, casting shimmering patterns across the walls. I select a high-quality whiskey, the rich amber liquid promising warmth and a false sense of camaraderie.

As I pour the drinks, my hands are steady, but inside, my nerves are taut as a bowstring. The vial of poison in my pocket feels like a lead weight pulling me down. My mind races, calculating every move, every potential slip that could give us away.

Behind me, Hawke continues to speak, his tone casual but with an undercurrent of menace. "You know, Marcus, I've been thinking about this partnership for a while. We could achieve great things together, expand our territories, increase our profits. No more unnecessary bloodshed."

Marcus's voice is equally smooth, but there's a hard edge to it. "I agree, Hawke. But let's not forget, this alliance is built on trust. And trust is something that's earned, not given."

I can feel Hawke's eyes on me as I finish pouring the drinks, keeping my back to his men. "Trust, yes. And loyalty," he adds, almost as an afterthought. "Loyalty is paramount."

I turn back to the table, carrying the tray with the three glasses. My steps are measured, my smile practiced. As I approach, Hawke's gaze narrows slightly, and I can sense his suspicion, his need to assert control.

"Thank you, my dear," Hawke says, taking one of the glasses from the tray. He studies me for a moment before raising his glass. "To new beginnings and prosperous ventures."

Marcus takes his glass as well, his eyes flicking to mine for the briefest second. "To mutual benefits," he says, clinking his glass against Hawke's.

As I step back, I feel the tension ratchet up another notch. I have to be careful, precise. No room for error.

Hawke raises his glass again, a mocking smile playing on his lips. "And to the lovely Kelsey, who will undoubtedly be the heart of this new alliance."

I force a laugh, feeling the weight of his gaze on me. "Thank you, Hawke. I'm just happy to be part of this."

As they bring their glasses to their lips, I hold my breath, waiting for the right moment. Hawke's eyes are on me, watching, assessing.

Marcus's eyes widen slightly, and I freeze, the color draining from my face. Hawke's smile widens, and he swaps his and Marcus's glasses around, his movements deliberate and slow.

"Let's see who luck favors tonight," he says, his gaze locking onto mine. "Did she want you dead or me? Did you trick her into believing there's warmth in that cold dead heart of yours?"

"You see, I enjoy a good gamble," Hawke continues, his tone light but tinged with menace. "And I like to keep things interesting. I saw you pour the poison, dear Kelsey. Two vials, I'm guessing one has nothing dangerous in it at all, but I'm a betting man. Life's more exciting with a bit of risk, don't you think?"

Marcus's jaw tightens, a flicker of anger crossing his face. He knows as well as I do that Hawke thrives on control and manipulation. The room feels like it's closing in, the air thick with tension.

Hawke picks up one of the glasses, swirling the amber liquid inside. "So, how about it?" he proposes, his voice dangerously smooth. "We each take a drink, and the two who live go into business together. Agreed? Does she want you dead or me?"

A heavy silence settles over the room, the weight of the decision pressing down on all of us. My gaze flickers between Marcus and Hawke, my mind racing.

Marcus meets my eyes, his expression hardening with

resolve. I nod once, a silent agreement to play this deadly game. He frowns but then he nods back.

Hawke, ever the showman, raises his glass in a mock toast, his eyes gleaming with malicious delight.

"To new beginnings," he says, his voice dripping with irony. "May the best man win."

We all raise our glasses, the clink of crystal echoing in the stillness. I can feel the weight of Marcus's gaze on me, his unspoken command to remain composed. My heart hammers in my chest as I bring the glass to my lips, the scent of whiskey sharp and overwhelming. The room seems to hold its breath as we each take a sip, liquid burning a fiery path down my throat.

For a moment, nothing happens. The world stands still, the only sound the faint clink of glasses being set back on the table. I feel a momentary surge of hope—maybe, just maybe, we've outplayed Hawke.

Marcus reaches for the necklace, his expression unreadable. He stumbles, clutching his chest with a pained gasp. The room erupts into chaos, Hawke's men springing to their feet, hands reaching for concealed weapons.

"Marcus!" I shout, rushing to his side as he collapses to the floor. His face contorts in pain, his breaths coming in ragged gasps.

Hawke's confusion morphs into a triumphant sneer. "Well, well," he says, stepping closer. "Looks like fate chose the best man."

His grin widens as he thanks me, revealing his true intentions. "You'll be my new sex slave, Kelsey. I'll keep you in the basement with all the others. Can't wait to see those juicy tits of yours."

A surge of fear and anger courses through me. "You're a monster," I spit, stepping back as he reaches for me. "I'll never be with you."

"Come, come, dear. We're in business together now. Your husband is dead. You inherit his wealth. You should be happy I'm not killing you as well for trying to poison me."

He reaches out, as if to claim me, but then he freezes, his expression twisting in shock. He staggers back, clutching his own chest.

"You... bitch," he gasps, fumbling for his gun. He points it my way but before he can pull the trigger, Marcus is on his feet, snatching it from him.

A cold silence descends on the room as Hawke's gasps turn to choking breaths. His men shift uncomfortably, their hands inching toward concealed weapons, but Marcus's men are quicker, guns already drawn and pointed.

Hawke's body convulses, his eyes wide with disbelief as he struggles for air. The poison takes hold swiftly, leaving him powerless, a once formidable man reduced to a gasping, helpless figure.

Marcus watches him with a cold, detached expression, a ruthless determination in his eyes. I can't tear my gaze away from the scene, my mind struggling to process the reality of what's happening.

The room is deathly quiet, the only sound Hawke's labored breathing growing fainter with each passing second.

Finally, with a last, shuddering breath, Hawke goes still. The life drains from his eyes, and his body slumps forward, lifeless. The tension in the room snaps, replaced by an eerie stillness.

Marcus steps forward, picking up the necklace from the table where Hawke had placed it. The diamonds sparkle coldly in the light, a symbol of the twisted game we had just played.

Marcus turns to me, his expression unreadable. "It's done," he says, his voice low and controlled.

He pockets the necklace, a grim satisfaction in his eyes. He glances around the room, his gaze sharp and commanding. "From now on, Hawke's territory belongs to me. Anyone who has a problem with that is free to leave—permanently."

"Someone go to the cellar," I demand, my voice shaking but firm. "Find out if he was telling the truth about sex slaves." Marcus nods to one of his men, who hurries to comply.

As they leave, Marcus pulls me into his arms. "Fate chose us to live," he says. "Wants us to have a family."

"Fate didn't get to choose," I reply. "I could tell he'd swap the glasses around, I made sure he saw me pour both vials."

"Why didn't you tell me what you had planned?"

I give him a wink. "Because you'd have told me not to do it."

He takes my hand, leading me from the room. "Dammit, you know me quite well, don't you?"

155

Once we're outside in the open air, he pulls out the necklace. "You should wear this."

"Really?"

"One moment." He flicks at the side of the biggest diamond in the necklace. "Still there. Good." The diamond opens like a box, revealing a tiny microchip inside.

"Decades of blackmail material," he continues, taking out the chip and slipping it into his inside jacket pocket. He clicks the diamond shut again. "He thought it just had sentimental value, dumb fuck. With that intel, he could have ruled the country, not just the city."

He slips the necklace around my neck. "When we get back, I'll swap the fake for the real diamond." He kisses my cheek.

"All this time," I say, sliding my hand along the necklace, "I thought it was just sentimental value."

"It is. It's also the most important thing I own. In many ways I shouldn't have kept the intel in there but I never expected some lucky asshole to come and steal it while my crew were upgrading the alarms. If he'd come ten minutes earlier or later, I'd have known about it and he'd never have gotten away."

I squeeze his hand. "But then we'd never have met." I reach up and kiss him. "Fate wanted this. Now we'll see if fate wants me to give you an heir."

TWENTY-SEVEN

Kelsey

Six months later...

Marcus holds my hand tightly, his thumb gently stroking the back of my hand. We've been waiting for this moment, and now that it's here, the swirl of emotions is overwhelming.

The door opens, and the doctor walks in, holding a folder. He's a middle-aged man with a kind smile that immediately puts me at ease.

"Good morning," he says warmly, taking a seat across from us. He opens the folder, glancing at the papers inside. "I have some good news for you both."

My breath catches in my throat, and I squeeze Marcus's hand. The anticipation is palpable. The doctor looks up, his smile widening. "Congratulations, you're definitely pregnant."

The words are like a beautiful explosion, filling the room

with a joy I can't quite describe. For a moment, I'm stunned, unable to fully process the reality of it.

I turn to Marcus, who looks equally shocked. His eyes are wide, but then they soften, and a slow, radiant smile spreads across his face.

He pulls me into a tight hug, his embrace filled with warmth and love. "We're going to be parents," he whispers.

Tears prick at the corners of my eyes, and I nod against his shoulder, the gravity of the moment sinking in. "I can't believe it," I say, my voice trembling.

There's a mix of fear and excitement swirling inside me, a cocktail of emotions that leaves me feeling both grounded and weightless.

The doctor gives us a moment before he continues. "Everything looks good so far. We'll want to schedule regular check-ups to monitor the pregnancy. It's important to stay healthy and stress-free."

He looks at Marcus, a knowing smile on his face. "That means keeping the work stress to a minimum."

Marcus chuckles, a sound filled with both relief and joy. "We'll do our best," he says, glancing at me with a twinkle in his eye. "I work from home a lot. Learning how to do video calls. Old dogs, new tricks."

I smile back, feeling a warmth spread through me. "Yeah, and my college has been really supportive. They've already talked about flexible scheduling and taking time off when needed."

The doctor nods approvingly. "That's good to hear. A supportive environment is crucial, especially during the early stages. And Marcus," he turns to him, "you're going to have an important role in this. Support, understanding, and, of course, being there every step of the way."

Marcus's grip on my hand tightens slightly, a silent promise. "I'm more than ready," he says, his voice firm but tender. "It seems to have taken forever to get here."

He looks back at me, his eyes filled with a depth of emotion that makes my heart flutter. "I can't wait to start shopping for baby things. I've been looking at cribs, car seats, everything. I want to make sure we have the best for our little one."

I laugh softly, feeling a lightness I haven't felt in a long time. "He sounds more excited than you," the doctor teases.

He grins, unashamed. "I might be. We're starting a family." He pauses, his expression softening. "And I want everything to be perfect."

The doctor's eyes twinkle with amusement. "It sounds like you two have everything under control. Just remember to take it one step at a time. The journey to parenthood is filled with surprises, but it's also incredibly rewarding."

As the doctor wraps up the appointment, giving us some final instructions and scheduling our next visit, I can't help but feel a sense of calm wash over me.

As we leave the office, Marcus keeps his arm around me, his protective nature more evident than ever. We walk out into the bright sunshine, the world seeming a little more vibrant, a little more hopeful.

He looks down at me, his expression soft and filled with

love. "We're really doing this," he murmurs, almost to himself. "We're going to be parents."

I nod, the reality settling comfortably in my chest. "Yeah, we are," I reply, feeling a rush of affection for the man beside me. "And I couldn't imagine doing it with anyone else."

He leans down, pressing a gentle kiss to my forehead. "Me neither," he whispers. "I love you, Kelsey."

"I love you too, Marcus," I whisper back, feeling a tear slip down my cheek.

"I've hired another chef, just to make sure you're getting all the nutrition you need and to cater to those cravings of yours."

I raise an eyebrow. "Another chef? We already have Chase."

He nods, a small smile playing on his lips. "I know, but this one's a specialist in pregnancy nutrition. I want to make sure you're eating the best possible meals. Healthy can still be delicious, you know."

I can't help but chuckle at his determination. "You really don't have to go through all this trouble."

Marcus's expression softens, and he reaches out to take my hand. "It's not trouble, Kelsey. I want to make sure you and the baby are healthy. Besides, I enjoy seeing you happy with your meals. It's a small price to pay."

I smile, feeling a mix of gratitude and amusement. "You're really going all out, aren't you?"

He squeezes my hand gently. "I just want to be prepared.

You and the baby mean everything to me, and I'll do whatever it takes to keep you both safe and healthy."

I look at him, touched by his dedication. "You're so attentive. It's... nice. Different from what I'm used to."

Marcus's eyes meet mine, full of sincerity. "Get used to it. I plan to be around and involved every step of the way. This is our family, and I'm going to make sure we have the best of everything."

His words make me feel incredibly cared for, and I can't help but lean in to kiss him softly. "Thank you, Marcus," I whisper, feeling a deep sense of comfort and security. "For everything."

TWENTY-EIGHT

Kelsey

Five months later...

The soft purr of Barney fills the living room as he curls up on my lap, content and oblivious to the world around him.

Marcus and I are sitting on the plush sofa watching Pretty Woman again, the warm glow of the fireplace casting a cozy light over us. It's one of those peaceful evenings where everything feels just right.

Marcus gently places his hand on my growing belly, his touch both protective and tender. I see the love in his eyes, a look that never fails to make my heart flutter.

The man who once seemed so distant and cold has become the center of my world, and the transformation in him is nothing short of miraculous.

"How's our little one doing today?" he asks, his voice soft and filled with wonder. His thumb gently strokes my skin, and I feel the baby respond with a slight kick. We both chuckle, marveling at the tiny life growing inside me.

"Active as ever," I reply, my hand resting over his. "I think she's going to be a little soccer player."

Marcus smiles, a mixture of pride and anticipation in his eyes. "She gets that from you, you know. All that determination and spirit."

I laugh, shaking my head. "Or maybe she's just as big a fighter as her father."

His expression turns thoughtful, the warmth in his eyes mingling with a hint of vulnerability.

It's clear what he's thinking. I reach up, cupping his face in my hands, my thumb brushing over his cheek.

"Marcus, you've already proven you're different from your father. You've absorbed Hawke's empire and kept it running smoothly without resorting to the same brutality. You've only made decisions that protect us, our family, and your people. You're not your father, and you never will be. You haven't even killed anyone for six months. That's got to be some kind of record."

"Came close with that delivery guy yesterday, music blasting from his truck like that."

"I'm glad you resisted. Otherwise how would we get the rest of the baby things delivered?"

Barney stretches, his purring intensifying as Marcus scratches behind his ears. It's a small, comforting sound that fills the room, adding to the warmth of the moment.

We sit there, lost in the comfort of each other's presence, the soft crackling of the fire and Barney's purring the only sounds in the room.

Marcus pulls me close, his eyes full of warmth and tenderness as he cups my face in his hands. His thumb gently strokes my cheek, and I feel a shiver of anticipation run through me.

He leans in, his lips capturing mine in a deep, passionate kiss that sends my heart racing. The world seems to melt away, leaving just the two of us in this perfect moment.

He gently places his hand on my growing belly, a mischievous glint in his eye. "You know, you're even more beautiful now."

I laugh softly, feeling a blush rise to my cheeks. "Even with all the changes and stretchmarks and stuff?"

"Especially with all the changes," he says, his voice full of sincerity. "You're glowing, and it's the most beautiful thing I've ever seen. Told you I wanted to see you like this, and you only get hotter by the day."

I bite my lip, touched by his words. "You're pretty hot yourself, you know."

He grins, leaning in to kiss me again. This time, the kiss is slower, more sensual. His hands slide down to my waist, pulling me closer as he deepens the kiss.

I feel a surge of desire, a craving for his touch that only grows stronger with each passing moment.

"Marcus," I whisper as we break the kiss, my voice breathless. "I need you."

He smiles, his eyes darkening with passion. "And I need you, Kelsey. Always." He lifts me gently, carrying me to the bedroom.

As he lays me down, his hands roam over my body, tracing every curve with reverence and care. I feel cherished, loved, and utterly safe in his arms.

He leans down, his lips brushing against my neck, sending shivers of pleasure down my spine. "You're so perfect," he murmurs against my skin, his voice full of awe. "I can't get enough of you."

I run my fingers through his hair, tugging him closer. "Then don't," I tease, my voice a mix of playfulness and desire. "I'm all yours."

He grins, capturing my lips in another searing kiss. As our clothes slowly come off, we take our time exploring each other, savoring the intimacy and connection we share.

As his hand slides over my stomach, he pauses, looking down at me with a gentle smile. "You and our baby are my world," he says softly. "I can't wait to meet our little one and start this new chapter of our lives."

Tears prick at the corners of my eyes, overwhelmed by the love and devotion I see in his eyes. "Me too," I whisper, my voice choked with emotion. "I'm so lucky to have you, Marcus."

He kisses me tenderly, his lips lingering on mine. "No, I'm the lucky one," he murmurs. "You've given me a reason to believe in love, to believe in a future. And I promise, I'll do everything I can to make you and our child happy."

The air between us crackles with anticipation, the electric current of desire building. I can feel his breath warm against my skin, his gaze intense and commanding.

"Strip for me," he murmurs, his voice low and demanding. It's not a request; it's an order, one that sends a thrilling shiver down my spine. I swallow hard, feeling both nervous and exhilarated by the idea.

Slowly, I begin to undress, my movements deliberate and teasing. I slide the straps of my dress off my shoulders, letting the fabric slip down my arms and pool at my feet.

I see the hunger in his eyes, the way he drinks in every inch of my exposed skin. His gaze is like a physical touch, setting my skin ablaze with desire.

I turn around, giving him a full view as I unhook my bra and let it fall away. I feel the cool air against my bare back, but the heat of his stare is even more intense.

I sway my hips slightly as I lower my panties, teasing him with the slow reveal of my body.

When I'm completely bare before him, I turn back to face him, my heart racing with a mix of vulnerability and excitement. Marcus's expression is one of pure lust and admiration, his eyes roaming over me with possessive appreciation.

"Come here," he commands, his voice a husky whisper. I step closer, my pulse quickening as he reaches out and pulls me onto his lap. His hands are warm and firm on my waist, guiding me to straddle him.

The intimacy of the position makes my breath hitch, the closeness of our bodies sending a wave of heat through me.

Marcus's hands glide up my sides, caressing my curves with a touch that is both gentle and demanding.

His fingers trace the outline of my breasts, making my

nipples harden under his touch. I gasp as he leans in, his lips brushing against my ear.

"You're mine," he whispers, his voice filled with possessive intensity. "Only mine."

His words send a jolt of pleasure straight to my core, and I can't help but moan softly. He smirks, clearly pleased with my reaction.

His hands move lower, skimming over my thighs and pulling me closer against him. I can feel his arousal pressing against me, a tangible reminder of his desire.

With a teasing grin, he leans back, his hands settling on my hips. "Show me how much you want this," he says, his tone challenging.

I bite my lip, feeling a surge of boldness. Slowly, I begin to move my hips, grinding against him in a sensual rhythm. The friction sends sparks of pleasure through me, and I can see the effect it's having on him. His jaw clenches, his eyes darkening even more with lust.

"Good girl," he praises, his hands tightening on my hips. "Just like that."

I continue to move, my body responding to his every touch, every word. The feeling of his hands on me, the sound of his voice, it's all driving me wild.

My breaths come faster, my moans growing louder as the pleasure builds.

Marcus's hands slide down to my thighs, his fingers brushing against my most sensitive spot. He teases me, his touch light and maddeningly slow. I whimper, my body arching towards him, silently begging for more.

"Please," I whisper, my voice trembling with need. "I need you."

He grins, clearly enjoying my desperation. "Not yet," he says, his voice low and commanding. "I want to hear you beg for it."

His fingers move in slow, torturous circles, pushing me closer and closer to the edge. The pleasure is overwhelming, consuming me. I can barely think, barely breathe, the only thing that matters is the feeling of his touch.

"Please, Marcus," I moan, my voice breaking. "Please, I need you so much."

He leans in, his lips brushing against mine in a teasing kiss. "That's my good girl," he murmurs, his voice a seductive purr. "Now, come for me."

With a final, skilled movement, he sends me over the edge. The orgasm crashes over me, powerful and all-consuming.

I cry out, my body trembling with the intensity of it. Marcus's hands hold me steady, his eyes never leaving mine.

As the waves of pleasure slowly subside, I collapse against him, my breath coming in ragged gasps. He strokes my back soothingly, his touch grounding me.

When I finally catch my breath, I look up at him, my eyes filled with love and desire. Marcus smiles, a tender, almost vulnerable expression on his face. He cups my cheek, his thumb brushing away a stray tear.

As we break apart, he gently lays me down on the bed, his eyes dark with desire.

"Now," he murmurs, his voice a low growl. "Let me show you just how much I love you."

Marcus's eyes are intense, locked onto mine as he thrusts deeply, filling me completely. The exquisite sensation sends waves of pleasure coursing through me, each movement a perfect blend of connection and ecstasy.

He slows his pace, his gaze never leaving mine, and leans down, his lips brushing against my ear.

"Touch yourself for me," he murmurs, his voice husky and commanding. The dominance in his tone sends a thrilling shiver through my body, igniting a fire deep within me.

My hand moves down my body. His rhythm intensifies, his thrusts deliberate and controlled, matching the growing intensity of my touch. His eyes darken with hunger, a growl of approval rumbling in his chest as I find my most sensitive spot.

"You're so perfect," he groans, his eyes fixed on my face, watching every flicker of pleasure that crosses it. "So beautiful, so mine."

His words are a catalyst, pushing me over the brink. My body tenses, a moan escaping my lips as another powerful orgasm crashes over me.

I tremble beneath him, my fingers still moving, prolonging the waves of bliss that pulse through me. Marcus's pace quickens, his control slipping as he watches me come undone beneath him.

"That's it," he growls, his voice thick with satisfaction. "Just like that, my love."

He thrusts harder, chasing his own release. I cling to him, feeling the tension in his body, the raw power of his desire.

As he reaches his peak, he groans my name, his voice filled with a mix of love and possession. He spills into me, the warmth of his release a final, perfect connection between us.

We collapse together, our bodies slick with sweat, hearts pounding in unison. He wraps his arms around me, pulling me close, his breath hot against my skin.

Marcus looks down at me, his eyes shining with love. "Thank you," he whispers, his voice full of emotion. "For loving me, for giving me this family."

I smile, reaching up to stroke his cheek as he pats my belly. "There's nothing I wouldn't do for you, Marcus. For all of us."

TWENTY-NINE

Marcus
_____

Four months later...

The conference room is silent as I take my seat at the head of the long, polished table.

The men around me are already deep in conversation, their voices a low hum as they discuss the latest developments.

My gaze is fixed on the necklace, in its case where it belongs. A link to the past, and the reason I have an heir for the future.

"Let's get started," I say, my voice firm and commanding. "We have a lot to cover today. Our first order of business is the integration of the last parts of Hawke's operations into our own. This is a significant move, and we need to ensure a smooth transition."

Carlo leans forward, his eyes sharp. "We've already absorbed the key territories. Our men have taken control of the docks and the warehouses. The supply lines are secure, but we're facing resistance from a few holdouts loyal to Hawke. They're trying to keep a foothold in the smuggling routes."

I nod, considering the information. "We can't allow any loose ends. Make it clear that they either work for us or they find themselves out in the cold. We need to solidify our control quickly and efficiently."

Another senior member speaks up. "What about the other factions? There are rumors that some are eyeing our expansion, considering it a sign of weakness or overreach. We need to ensure they understand that this is our territory now."

I meet his gaze, my expression hardening. "We'll deal with them in due time. For now, focus on consolidating our gains. If anyone challenges us, they will be met with force. Make it clear that any move against us will be met with swift retaliation. This is our city, and we won't tolerate any threats."

The men nod in agreement, their expressions resolute. They know the stakes and the importance of maintaining a strong, unified front.

There's a confidence in the room, born from our most recent victories and the strength of our leadership. But there's also an undercurrent of unease, a recognition that we're navigating dangerous waters.

As we continue to discuss the logistics of the takeover, my phone buzzes on the table, vibrating softly against the wood. I glance down at the screen and see a message from Kelsey: *It's time.*

My heart skips a beat, a mix of excitement and anxiety flooding my system. I stand, the room quieting instantly as I do. All eyes are on me, waiting for my next words.

"Gentlemen, I have to step out," I announce, my voice steady. "Continue with the plans and ensure that everything is set in motion. I expect full reports by the end of the day."

Carlo nods. "Understood, Marcus. We'll take care of it."

I nod back, satisfied that everything is under control. I trust my men implicitly; they know their roles and the importance of this moment. Carlo's been nothing but loyal since I broke his fingers.

As I step into the hallway, I pull out my phone and quickly call the driver, instructing him to be ready.

I glance back at the conference room door, knowing that while one chapter is closing, another is just beginning. The empire I've built, the power I've amassed, none of it compares to the life awaiting me with Kelsey and our child.

I find Kelsey pacing the living room, her face a mixture of pain and determination. "Marcus, it's happening," she says, her voice trembling but strong. "Had to be during your meeting, didn't it?"

"I don't give a shit about that." I wrap my arms around her, my presence a calming force. "I'm here, Kelsey. We'll get through this together."

I get her out to the waiting car, holding her hand the entire time, bags over my shoulder.

Kelsey grips my fingers tightly, her knuckles white from the force. I try to keep my voice calm, whispering words of encouragement, though inside, I'm just as anxious as she is.

"You're doing great, Kelsey," I murmur, squeezing her hand. "Just a little longer, and we'll meet our baby."

She flashes me a strained smile, her face pale but determined. "I can't believe it's finally happening," she says, her voice breathless. "I'm not sure I can do this, Marcus."

I lean in closer, brushing a stray hair from her forehead. "Sure you can. Piece of cake, trust me. Won't be in the hospital long."

She chuckles, though it's more a release of tension than actual humor. "In and out in two minutes, like sex with you."

We share a moment of quiet laughter, the kind that eases the nerves just a bit.

As the hospital comes into view, the seriousness of the situation settles over us again.

The car screeches to a halt, and we quickly make our way inside, Kelsey clutching her belly with one hand and my arm with the other.

The emergency room is a whirlwind of activity, but the staff recognizes the urgency and importance of our arrival.

They move us swiftly to a private room, the hustle and bustle of the hospital fading behind closed doors. Nurses and doctors flit around us, preparing for the imminent arrival.

I stay close to Kelsey, never letting go of her hand. Her

eyes lock onto mine, and I see a mixture of fear and determination there. I lean down, kissing her forehead.

"You're the strongest person I know," I whisper. "We've got this."

She nods, a tear escaping her eye. "I know. I just... I'm scared, Marcus."

I tighten my grip on her hand. "I'm here," I say, my voice low. "We're in this together, every step of the way. Like we agreed."

The hours stretch on, each one feeling longer than the last. Kelsey's contractions grow more intense, her face contorted in pain. She grits her teeth, fighting through each wave with a fierce resolve that leaves me in awe.

"Remember that time we took down Hawke's entire operation in one night? That was tough, right?"

She laughs weakly, shaking her head. "Yeah, because I had backup that time. This is all me."

I lean in, my voice serious. "I've seen you outmaneuver a mafia boss and survive. You got justice for Maria. You can do this."

She smiles, but it's clear the pain is wearing her down. The doctor checks her progress, nodding in approval. "It's almost time," he announces. "Just a few more pushes, Kelsey. You're doing great."

Kelsey lets out a long breath, squeezing my hand with surprising strength. "Marcus," she says, her voice strained, "I need you to keep talking. Distract me."

I nod, scrambling for something to say. "Remember our last date night?" I start, a smile tugging at my lips. "You wore that red dress, the one that made my brain short-circuit. I couldn't take my eyes off you."

She snorts, then winces as another contraction hits. "Yeah, and it didn't fit me at all with this belly in it"

I smile. "Still looked gorgeous in it."

She nods, tears streaming down her face. With a final, guttural cry, she pushes one last time, and then... the sound of a baby crying fills the room.

The doctor lifts our baby, announcing, "It's a girl!"

Kelsey collapses back against the bed, tears of relief and joy in her eyes. I feel my own eyes sting as I look at our daughter, tiny and perfect in the doctor's hands.

They place her on Kelsey's chest, and I watch, utterly captivated, as she takes her first breaths.

Kelsey looks up at me, her face glowing with an exhausted but radiant smile. "We did it," she whispers, her voice choked with emotion.

I nod, unable to speak past the lump in my throat. I lean down, pressing a kiss to her forehead, then one to our daughter's tiny head. "You both did amazing," I finally manage, my voice thick.

As the nurses clean up and the doctor gives us space, I sit beside Kelsey, our daughter cradled between us. We stare at her, utterly enraptured by this little life we've brought into the world.

In the quiet that follows, Kelsey looks at me, her eyes soft and full of love. "Marcus, thank you... for everything."

I shake my head, feeling overwhelmed by the depth of my feelings for her. "No, thank you, Kelsey. You've given me more than I ever thought possible."

She looks down at our daughter, her eyes shining with a mix of exhaustion and joy. "She's perfect," she whispers, her voice filled with awe.

I lean in, pressing a gentle kiss to Kelsey's forehead and then to our daughter's. "You both are," I say softly, my heart swelling with love and pride.

Her voice breaks. "Welcome to the world, little Maria. We're going to give you the best life possible."

THIRTY

Marcus

Five years later...

Our lives have settled into a beautiful rhythm. Kelsey is well on the way to becoming a doctor, and I couldn't be prouder of her.

Our little Maria is thriving, and I've managed to balance my responsibilities with the joy of fatherhood and partnership. Even got the hang of video calls.

Today, I sit in my favorite armchair, the soft leather creaking slightly as I shift my weight. The room is filled with the quiet hum of voices, my men standing around me, waiting for their instructions.

Barney is sprawled across my lap, purring contentedly as I absentmindedly stroke his fur. It's a strange juxtaposition— this peaceful domesticity against the backdrop of a once tumultuous empire, now fully absorbed and under my control.

I look around me. The room looks more homely, Kelsey's touch at work. I never gave a shit about how my place looked but now, bookcases are full, paintings on the wall, it just seems right.

"Alright," I begin, my voice steady and authoritative. "Let's go over today's agenda." I glance around the room, meeting the eyes of each man in turn.

They're loyal, disciplined, and know the weight of the responsibilities they carry. "First order of business: the shipments. I want everything to run like clockwork. No delays, no mishaps. Make sure the shipment arrives on time. No excuses."

There's a murmur of agreement, pens scratching against notepads as they jot down the details. The takeover of Hawke's empire was not without its challenges, but we've come out stronger, more unified.

Now, it's a matter of maintaining control and ensuring that every cog in this machine functions smoothly longterm.

"And about the distribution network," I continue, leaning forward slightly. "I want tighter security measures. We can't afford any leaks. Double the guards if necessary. I don't want any surprises."

One of the men, Alex, nods and makes a note. "We'll handle it, boss," he says, his voice firm with conviction. "No one's getting through our defenses."

I give a curt nod, satisfied with his response. "Good. Remember, our reputation depends on efficiency and reliability. We've taken over Hawke's operations completely, but that doesn't mean we can slack off. We need to prove we're better, stronger. Understood?"

A chorus of "Yes, boss" echoes through the room, the men straightening their postures. They know what's at stake, and they're ready to deliver.

"And I have one more item on the agenda, top priority."

They wait for me to continue.

"The bookstore is due a fresh batch of Marian Keyes. Make sure it arrives without the boxes damaged this time or heads will roll."

I dismiss them with a wave of my hand. They gather their things, ready to head out and execute the day's tasks.

I clear my throat, catching their attention one last time. "One more thing," I add, my tone casual but commanding. "I have a medical appointment in this room. I am not to be disturbed for at least four hours, understood?"

There's a brief pause, a flicker of curiosity in their eyes, but none of them dare to ask. They know better than to pry into my personal life. Instead, they nod in unison, their expressions respectful.

"Of course, boss," Tony replies, speaking for the group. "We'll take care of everything."

I nod in acknowledgment, watching as they file out of the room, their footsteps fading down the hall. The door closes behind them, leaving me alone with Barney, who stretches luxuriously in my lap.

I lean back in the chair, a deep sense of contentment settling over me.

The silence in the room is comforting, a stark contrast to the chaos and violence that once defined my days.

Absorbing Hawke's empire was a monumental task, fraught with danger and bloodshed.

But now, with the power consolidated under my control, there's a sense of stability—a foundation upon which we can build something enduring.

I glance down at the cat, who looks up at me with half-lidded eyes. "You know, Barney," I murmur, scratching behind his ears, "life has a funny way of turning out, doesn't it? Who would've thought we'd end up here waiting for the best doctor in the world to attend to me?"

I stand, carefully lifting Barney from my lap and placing him on the floor. He looks up at me, seemingly annoyed at being disturbed, before padding off out of the room to find another spot to nap.

Kelsey walks in a moment later, a playful smile on her face. She's wearing a large coat that seems out of place for the warm weather. I raise an eyebrow.

"Hey, beautiful. What's with the coat?" I ask, a smirk playing on my lips.

"Maria is at school for a few more hours," she says, her eyes twinkling with mischief. With a dramatic flourish, she opens the coat to reveal a sexy doctor's uniform under-neath. "Happy birthday, Marcus," she adds, her voice sultry and teasing. "Time for your medical."

She looks absolutely stunning, and the sight of her in that outfit sends a rush of desire through me. "Looks like I really do need that medical appointment."

She steps closer, her fingers trailing lightly over my chest. "I think you might be right. Let's see what's wrong with you," she says, playing along with a serious expression that doesn't quite mask her amusement.

I groan theatrically, placing a hand over my chest. "Doctor, I think I'm injured. I might need a thorough examination."

Her eyes darken with desire as she slips into her role. "Well, we can't have that, can we? Let's get you checked out," she says, her voice low and intimate.

She begins her "examination," her hands moving over my body with exaggerated care. Each touch is a tease, igniting a fire within me. Her fingers trail over my chest, my abs, and lower, making me ache for more.

"How does this feel?" she asks, her voice a seductive whisper as she runs her hand over my thigh.

"Good, Doctor. But I think the pain is somewhere... higher," I reply, my breath hitching as her hand moves closer to where I want it most.

With a wicked smile, she unbuckles my belt and pulls down my pants, revealing my growing arousal. She gives me a mock-serious look. "This looks very serious. I'll need to examine it up close."

She holds a stethoscope around her neck and a mischievous sparkle in her eye, clearly enjoying the role she's playing.

She taps her chin thoughtfully, biting back a smile. "I believe the patient requires a more thorough examination," she says in a mock-serious tone, her voice a perfect blend of authority and seduction.

She steps closer, her fingers gently brushing my chest as she begins unbuttoning my shirt. Each button she undoes sends a shiver of anticipation through me.

"Let's see," she murmurs, slipping her hands inside my shirt to caress my bare skin. "Heart rate seems a bit elevated. Do you feel anxious, sir?"

I chuckle, trying to keep my composure as her hands explore my chest. "More like... excited," I admit, my voice low and husky. "Doctor, I need to know exactly what's causing it."

She grins, a devilish glint in her eyes. "Well, let's see," she says, dropping her voice to a whisper. She leans in, her lips brushing against mine before she moves down to kiss my neck. She lingers there, teasingly biting and licking, making me groan in pleasure.

Her hands move lower, undoing my belt and sliding it off with a tantalizing slowness that has me aching for her. She strips me down to my underwear, every movement deliberate, her eyes locked on mine.

The anticipation is killing me, and she knows it. I can see the satisfaction in her gaze as she takes her time, savoring the power she has over me.

Finally, she kneels in front of me, her hands gliding up my thighs. She leans in, her breath hot against my skin, and I shudder.

"Doctor," I gasp, barely able to keep control, "please, touch me."

She smirks, clearly enjoying the effect she's having on me. "I'm sorry, sir," she says, her voice dripping with playful mockery. "But I haven't completed the examination yet. Time for a temperature check."

Her mouth slips over my cock. I can't help but groan as she takes me in her mouth, her tongue doing things that make me see stars.

She's merciless, teasing me with her mouth, her tongue swirling and flicking in ways that drive me insane. She pulls back occasionally, her eyes meeting mine with a wicked smile, only to dive back in, drawing out the pleasure until I'm nearly begging for release. "Seems very hot," she says, slapping my cock onto her cheeks.

My hands tangle in her hair, holding on as she works her magic, my breaths coming in ragged gasps as she shoves my shaft to the back of her throat.

"Doctor," I manage to choke out, my voice strained with need. "Please, I can't take it anymore."

She pulls back, her lips glistening, her eyes gleaming with satisfaction. "I think you're ready for the next part of my treatment."

She points a finger at me, mock-serious. "This isn't just you objectifying me because I'm nearly qualified, is it?"

"Maybe a little," I reply, unable to keep the grin off my face.

"Oh, good." She grins back, clearly pleased with herself. She moves closer, and I pull her onto my lap, capturing her mouth in a deep, hungry kiss.

Our tongues dance together, and I can feel the heat of her body against mine, the softness of her curves.

With a quick movement, she stands and begins a slow strip-tease, her eyes never leaving mine. She sways her hips, teasing me with every inch of skin she reveals.

The top comes off first, revealing her lace bra. Then she unzips her skirt, letting it drop to the floor. She steps out of it, standing before me in just her lingerie, the sight of her almost too much to bear.

"You're driving me crazy," I groan, my eyes raking over her body.

She smirks, clearly enjoying herself. "Good," she purrs. "Now, lie down. It's time to make you better."

I do as she says, lying back on the plush rug. She straddles me, her hands on my chest, leaning down to kiss me again. Her hair falls around us like a curtain.

She sits up, her hands moving to her bra, unhooking it and letting it fall away. My hands immediately go to her breasts, cupping them, feeling their softness.

"You're perfect," I whisper, my voice thick with desire.

She smiles, a flush of pleasure on her cheeks. "The prescription," she says, her voice low and sultry, "is coming inside my pussy. Do you consent to that course of treatment?"

"Absolutely," I breathe, my hands gripping her hips.

She reaches down, guiding me to her entrance. Slowly, she sinks back down onto me, both of us gasping at the sensation. She starts moving, her rhythm slow and deliberate, driving me crazy with every roll of her hips.

Her hands rest on my chest, her nails digging into my skin as she rides me, her movements graceful and sensual.

"Touch yourself," I command, my voice rough with need.

She bites her lip, her eyes dark with desire. She slides a hand between us, her fingers finding her clit. The sight of her touching herself, the pleasure on her face, nearly pushes me over the edge.

She moans, her hips grinding against me, and I can feel her tightening around me.

"That's it," I murmur, my hands on her hips, guiding her movements. "Come for me, baby. Show me how much you love this."

Her breaths come faster, her movements more frantic. "Marcus," she gasps, her voice trembling with pleasure. "I love you. I love this. Oh, God..."

Her orgasm hits her hard, her body convulsing around me. I hold her steady, thrusting up into her as she rides out her climax, her cries of pleasure music to my ears. The sight of her, the feel of her, the sound of her moans—it all pushes me to the brink.

With a final, deep thrust, I come, the pleasure crashing over me like a tidal wave. I bury myself inside her, feeling the heat of her body around me, the perfect completion of our connection.

We stay like that for a moment, our bodies intertwined, our breaths mingling as we come down from the high.

"You're perfect," I whisper again, my voice filled with awe. "You're mine."

She leans down, kissing me fiercely. "I'm yours," she agrees, her voice breathless. "Always."

THIRTY-ONE

Kelsey

The penthouse, now filled with warmth and love, feels worlds away from the cold, impersonal space it used to be.

My heart swells as I glance around at the photos of our little family adorning the walls.

My eyes settle on the clock. She's due home any moment. I close my textbooks ready for her arrival.

As if on cue, the door opens, and Mrs. Johnson, our housekeeper, steps inside with Maria in tow.

Maria's face lights up when she sees us, and she runs toward us, her little feet pattering on the polished floor.

"Mommy! Daddy! Look what I made at school!" she exclaims, holding up a colorful painting of our family.

I kneel down to her level, taking the painting in my hands. "It's beautiful, sweetheart. You did such a great job," I say, my voice filled with pride.

Marcus scoops Maria up into his arms, spinning her around. Her giggles fill the room, a sound that never fails to bring a smile to my face.

"You're becoming quite the artist, Maria. Should we do some more painting together?" he asks, his eyes twinkling.

Maria nods enthusiastically. "Yes, please, Daddy!"

I watch them, feeling a warmth spread through my chest. Seeing Maria so happy and loved, I can't help but think about my own childhood. The stark contrast between her life and mine is staggering.

Maria has never heard raised voices or felt the sting of a hit. She's growing up surrounded by love, security, and the knowledge that she's cherished.

"Mommy, come look!" Maria calls, pulling me out of my thoughts.

I join them on the couch, Maria still perched on Marcus's lap, holding her painting proudly. "Tell me about your day, Maria. What else did you do at school?" I ask, brushing a stray lock of hair from her face.

"We made animal masks, and I was a lion! Rawr!" she says, making a fierce face that melts into giggles.

Marcus laughs, kissing the top of her head. "My fierce little lion. Did you scare all your friends?"

Maria shakes her head, her eyes bright with happiness. "No, Daddy. We all wore masks and had a parade! It was so much fun."

I wrap my arms around both of them, my heart overflowing with love and contentment. As I hold them close, I silently vow to keep this happiness alive, to ensure that Maria never knows the pain and fear I endured.

We move to the large kitchen table, where Marcus sets out paints, brushes, and a fresh canvas for Maria. He helps her into a little apron, and they start working on a new master-piece together. I lean against the doorway, watching them with a soft smile.

"Daddy, can you paint a sun for me?" Maria asks, her big eyes full of trust and admiration.

"Of course, sweetheart," Marcus replies, dipping a brush into the yellow paint. He carefully paints a bright sun in the corner of the canvas while Maria works on a colorful garden below.

Their interaction is heartwarming, and I marvel at the ease with which Marcus embraces his role as a father.

Love has softened him, and it shows in every gentle stroke of the brush and every word of praise he gives Maria.

"You're doing great, Maria," I say, joining them at the table. "Your garden looks beautiful."

Maria beams at me. "Thanks, Mommy! Do you want to paint with us?"

I nod, taking a seat beside her. "I'd love to." I pick up a brush and start adding flowers to her garden, the three of us working together in perfect harmony.

As we paint, I can't help but think about my own child-hood again. My father never spent time like this with me. He was always too busy with his schemes and anger. I push the thought away, focusing on the happiness of the present.

Marcus looks up at me, his eyes filled with warmth. "You know, Kelsey, I never thought I'd enjoy painting this much," he says with a chuckle. "But doing it with you two makes it perfect."

I smile at him, my heart swelling with love. "You're a natural, Marcus. Maria's lucky to have such a talented daddy."

When the painting is finished, Maria stands back to admire our work. "It's so pretty! Can we hang it in my room?"

"Absolutely," Marcus says, lifting her up so she can see the canvas better. "It's a masterpiece."

I nod in agreement. "We'll hang it right where you can see it every day."

Maria wraps her arms around Marcus's neck, hugging him tightly. "Thank you, Daddy."

He hugs her back, his eyes meeting mine over her shoulder. "Anything for you, my little artist."

As we clean up the painting supplies, I can't help but feel a deep sense of contentment. This is the life I always dreamed of for my family—filled with love, support, and the freedom to express ourselves.

Maria will never know the pain and fear that I did. She will grow up knowing she is loved and cherished every single day.

———

AS THE SUN begins to set, we gather around the dining table for dinner. Chase, our private chef, has outdone himself tonight.

The aroma of roasted chicken, garlic mashed potatoes, and freshly baked bread fills the air. Maria's eyes light up at the sight of her favorite meal.

"Chase, this smells amazing!" I say, smiling at him as he places the last dish on the table.

"Thank you, Kelsey. I hope you all enjoy it," he replies, returning my smile before heading back to the kitchen.

We sit down, and Marcus helps Maria with her napkin, tucking it neatly into her shirt. She giggles, her excitement palpable. "I love chicken! Thank you, Chase!" she calls out.

Chase pokes his head back in, grinning. "You're welcome, Maria. Enjoy!"

As we finish the main course and move on to dessert—homemade apple pie—I decide to broach a topic that's been on my mind. "Maria, what would you think about having a baby brother or sister?"

Her eyes widen with excitement. "Really? A baby? Can I help take care of them?"

Marcus and I exchange a warm glance. "Of course, sweetheart," Marcus says, reaching over to ruffle her hair. "You'd be a great big sister."

Maria nods eagerly. "I promise to help with everything! Diapers, feeding, playing...everything!"

I chuckle, touched by her enthusiasm. "We know you will, Maria. And we'll all work together as a family."

Marcus reaches for my hand, squeezing it gently. "You've been amazing, Kelsey. Balancing work and everything else. I don't know how you do it."

I smile, feeling the warmth of his words. "I have a great support system. Between you, Maria, and Chase, I feel like I can do anything."

Barney meows from the corner of the room. "And you," I add as Maria giggles."

Marcus looks at me over Maria's head, his eyes soft with love. "You know, Kelsey, I never thought I'd have this. A family, a home filled with so much love. You've given me more than I ever dreamed possible."

I lean in, kissing him softly. "We've given it to each other, Marcus. This is our life, and it's beautiful."

Marcus kisses me gently. "Speaking of the future...what do you think about starting on that baby brother or sister tonight?"

I laugh softly, pulling him towards me. "I think that sounds perfect."

9 798223 295389